CW00857886

HOW TO ATTRACT ARMCHAIR

INVESTORS FOR PROPERTY

A guide to successfully finding private
investors who'll fund your property deals

Tim Matcham

Acknowledgements

My loving wife Vikki and our four gorgeous children

Tim Fox Evans, Photographer – cover photo

Mike Knight

Jo Rogers

Mark Barratt

Stephanie Hale

My existing clients, may you continue to thrive!

To my future clients – success is within reach, just take the next step!

What Other People Are Saying

"Tim was very helpful on transition of our business when we were in overwhelm. He helped us prioritise, focus and communicate better, and seemed to have an army of helpful tools and techniques at his fingertips. A lovely calm and measured approach helped clarify issues and move us forwards."

John & Bronwen Vearncombe

"Tim's coaching is truly excellent, he has really helped me focus on what's important in my business. I'd say he's probably saved me 8 months worth of misdirected effort. His calm and considered style of coaching, coupled with his extensive knowledge and experience, is perfect for teasing the correct and most appropriate course of action out of you. He has certainly guided me away from the mass of detail and refocused my attention towards the end state. Even after a few sessions I have regained my focus and have a sound plan of action to achieve my goals. Highly recommended."

Grantley Clapham

"Ike and I have had the pleasure of having Tim as one of our property mentors for the past few months. We have now secured ourselves a mortgage option that would save us over £11K in comparison to the bridging finance we originally thought we needed, because Tim shared one of his contacts who sat with us to analyse all possible finance options.

We are particularly impressed by the way he took his time to understand our situation when we first met and came up with a more viable mentoring approach which is completely different to what we thought was possible.

No matter how tense or discouraged we felt, Tim made sure he pointed out the massive progress we've made – and we end up leaving every meeting with a smile. Tim would be a great asset to any power team!"

Ike and Toyosi Jagun

"Tim really helped and supported me in structuring a formula for raising finance to continue building my property portfolio. It was something I had never done before and I was a bit daunted about how to start and go about it.

He gave me great advice about how to approach different types of investors. He also showed me how to make sure I had everything in place to be able to answer the different questions investors may ask and also be able to reassure them that their money was safe with a competent and trustworthy person/company.

As a result I have had success in approaching and talking to several investors and am well on the way to raising the finance I need for several projects I am involved in.

Tim is very approachable and easy to talk to. He gave me the confidence I needed to go out of my comfort zone, and helped me to see the value in what I had to offer to potential investors.

I would recommend Tim to anyone who may be finding certain aspects of finding investor finance challenging. He has a proven track record and a system that works!"

Niki Breeze

CONTENTS

INTRODUCTION
How To Leverage Other People's Money

So, you want to work on a property deal? Good idea! Property investing is a smart way to get some really great returns, when you know what you're doing.

Of course, investing in property requires money, and regardless of how much you may have, sooner or later, you'll run out of it. At this point, you'll either need to wait for your investment to grow significantly to "get your money back out" … or leverage other people's money.

From a recent survey of property investors, the two biggest hurdles (by far) for most property investors and developers are simply:

1. Finding the right deals so that the investment is attractive and that the "numbers stack up".

2. Getting hold of enough money to secure the property.

I'm assuming that number (1) is already either taken care of, or you're working on it. The challenge is that great deals don't come around very often, and when they do, you'll have to act fast because the vendor is usually stressed and needs a quick sale. Plus, your competitors will not wait around, and a delay will likely cost you the opportunity which will be snapped up elsewhere, which is frustrating, needless, and may impact on other deals you may receive.

When you're experienced in leveraging other people's money, you have access to an almost limitless amount of investment capital which will enable you to:

1. **Move quickly and secure the great deals.** Having money

at your disposal means you can move fast and secure deals before it's too late.

2. **Get properties cheaper.** Being able to offer cash to vendors – fast – is a powerful motivator.

3. **Get bigger deals.** Remember, you're not limited to only what you can afford ... think big!

4. **Get better deals.** Again, having money behind you will eliminate a lot of your competition so you can have better deals outside their scope.

5. **Compound your results.** As your reputation for being able to finance deals gets around, you'll get access to more deals, better deals ... it's a virtuous cycle.

6. **Access other people's expertise and support.** Often, investors will offer ideas and help. (After all – they want their investment to succeed.)

In short, having access to private investor finance means that your only limits are your time, imagination, and competence in completing projects. You can become successful and financially free far quicker when your access to cash is unlimited via leverage.

Who exactly is this book for?

This book is for people who understand that property can provide you with time freedom. It's not so much about retirement: this is about valuing time and understanding that you have a choice with your time.

Property, though, as we know, is expensive. It doesn't really matter how much of your own money you've got, whether that's a few tens of thousands, hundreds of thousands or even nothing at all (that's where I started). At some point, you're going to run out, and the people that I'm looking at for this book are people who've perhaps invested in gaining some knowledge about property. Maybe you have taken the first steps, and perhaps you are starting to build your portfolio and working towards your own financial freedom, but have hit a barrier, and that barrier is that you've run out of your own money.

In order to take the next step, and to progress on your property journey and to achieve the kind of goals that you're looking to achieve, you need to start working with other people's money; investors who are interested in getting a better return on their investment. But – and it's a big "but" – particularly in the UK, we have a real stigma attached to talking about money, and about asking people for money.

So I've devised this programme and articulated in this book that it's not really about asking for money. It's about framing it in a different way and adopting the right mindset so that we are presenting an opportunity; we are addressing investors' fears and concerns and answering their pain points and the challenges that they face, providing everybody involved with an opportunity to benefit from working together.

So you, the property investor, benefits because you're able to enlarge your portfolio, and private investors benefit because they're getting significantly better return than they would have done had they left that money in a bank or building society, and they're not riding the vagaries of the stock market which, as we know, can go up and down.

So I'm aiming to provide you with an alternative means of gaining finance and the understanding that if it's presented in the right way, this can benefit all parties. If it's done professionally and properly, you can work together with private investors for mutual benefit.

"With wind in her sails you can take a sailing boat anywhere. Provide that energy and I can take you where you want to go."

Is this book for beginners or more experienced property investors?

This book is for everybody on their property journey, whether they are just starting out or whether they are more experienced. For you, if you are just starting out, this book will give you encouragement that significant progress is possible. That you can build a significant portfolio without having to wait until you have your own funds available. When I started, I had absolutely no funds at all!

For you, if you are more experienced, this book will enable you to accelerate your journey and consider larger more profitable deals that you might otherwise not have considered.

I think it's important here that we understand that property is a business. This book isn't really for accidental landlords and people who are sort of dabbling at the periphery of property. This is for you if you are serious about running this as a business and taking it forward in a professional way with professional teams and advisers.

People often say to me, "Well, I can't invest in property because I haven't got any money." Let me tell you about my first investment property: I had minus about £100,000. That didn't stop me from taking the steps necessary in order to acquire and work on property, and benefit from property, so these excuses of "I haven't got any money" are just exactly that, they are excuses. They are people putting up barriers unnecessarily in some instances. There are ways of buying property and working with property without necessarily having your own funds available, and the whole purpose of this book is to show you that, with the right approach, it doesn't matter whether you have or haven't got money. There are ways of building your property portfolio. So, even if you are a beginner, there are possibilities for you.

Case Study 1

When I first started out, I had no money available for investing in property. Worse than that, I had previously invested in a couple of projects that I hadn't had control of, and they didn't work out quite as planned. I have since rescued them but was licking my wounds a little to start with.

The plan was to purchase a large building and convert the space into multiple units. Splitting the space up would give us a potentially greater return as well as the refurbishment. The property, in the centre of Cheltenham, was purchased using a combination of bridging finance and investors' finance, meaning we didn't need to use any of our own cash (which we didn't have anyway!). The purchase price was £300,000 and was sold for £750,000 after about 18 months, allowing repayment of all the various loans.

So we created something out of nothing using none of our own money at all, and it shows that just because you haven't got any money, doesn't mean to say you can't invest in property.

Having said that, some of the people that I work with are very experienced. At first glance, I sometimes wonder how much value I can add to their particular proposition. It's not until I start digging deeper that I realise that whilst they've maybe got 90 per cent of what they need in order to work in the private investor arena, there are a few things that need to be addressed to get everything in alignment so that a whole new world opens up.

The missing 10 per cent

Let me tell you about the missing 10 per cent. This is going to be different for everybody. The whole idea here is that learning new skills can be quite daunting when you first start. But if you're like most property investors I know, you probably have most of the ingredients you need already in place. Think of it this way: if you've got a pin code for a credit card and you punch in one wrong number, it might only be one digit out, but you're not going to gain access because it's not the right code. Similarly, if you've got a padlock or a safe with multiple digits, you've only got to have one element of it one click out, and that's sufficient for you not to be able to unlock the potential of what is there. You only need that missing digit to unlock everything you need.

To give you another metaphor: I was having a discussion recently with a client about interlocking Chinese metal ring puzzles, where you've got rings that are seemingly attached together, and you pull and you push at them, and you can't open the puzzle up. If you get the alignment absolutely dead right, they slide apart without any effort at all. You know that you can do it, and you've seen maybe other people do it, but you haven't quite got the alignment right so it's not quite working for you. You can waste a lot of energy and effort and get very frustrated because you can't do it. The more you tug and pull at it, the more frustrating and the worse it gets. But once you know the secret, and it unlocks, it's a very simple, easy process, and it just glides apart.

This is what I want you to achieve by reading this book. The first step is about identifying where your blockers are and what's holding you back and then addressing each of these individually so that we can get the combination right to help you unlock your natural talents.

How I can help you?

In the world of property education, there's a huge amount of education for all the different types of strategies. Many strategies come and go regarding popularity of what's possible and in terms of great cash flow or capital growth or making money. Those areas are covered in abundance by a lot of people who are very knowledgeable and very skilful in what they do, but frequently the finance side of it is almost an aside.

It's almost suggested that, "If you find a great deal, you will find the money." People are feeling like they're being fobbed off by that, and it's a real mental block in their heads. They recognise that it's something that is holding them back, and without unlocking that element of it, they're really going to be stuck in what they're doing. They might have to wait until they can release more equity from the properties that they've got, or wait until perhaps in their day job, if they're still working, they've earned sufficient to be able to buy the next property. So they can keep growing their property portfolio, but it's going to be a very much slower process.

As I said at the beginning of this book, this is about gaining time freedom to allow you the choice to be able to do what you want when you want to do it. If you want to help people, it may be for charity or to spend time with your family, or to help out in whatever way is appropriate for you.

Property has the potential to be able to do that, providing you follow the rules; get yourself educated and continue to learn about all the different strategies and build a power team around you of people that can help and guide you.

This is about adding another string to your bow in terms of help and guidance, allowing you to progress faster and with more confidence than you would have done if you'd not been able to have access to that.

So how will this book help you?

I'm confident that this book will help pretty much everybody. It will help you to understand that this is about offering opportunity – it's not the begging or asking for money as so many people seem to fear. Brits, in particular, seem to have a barrier about talking about money, but I will show you that this isn't talking about the money, it's talking about the opportunity and how this can benefit people. I'll show you that just by changing your mindset and looking at it from a different perspective, it will help you to overcome your own limiting beliefs and see that there is another way that you can do this that's not aggressive, underhand, or salesy.

You don't have to be a salesman. Perhaps you might think that's what you have to be to raise private finance; you may think you have to sell something, or have to be smooth talking. But none of these things are true.

I will help you to understand what it is that private investors are looking for and how you can use your own skill set to achieve this. Just because you don't have skills that you perceive as being necessary, doesn't mean you can't harness the skills that you already do have. What I will help you to do is to identify the things that you are really good at, so that people will come to you because of the value you offer.

The fact that you are likely to be different from the next person is fantastic and to be celebrated, rather than something to worry about or be concerned with. In fact, I think it's quite key. You may think, "Oh well, I haven't got this or I haven't got that," so you fear you lack the necessary skills to raise private finance. My book will help you to start seeing that you have positive qualities that will help to achieve what you want. You just need to gain confidence in your own abilities.

Sometimes, you're too close to be able to see it yourself. So my book will help you to understand that you do have value and can do this.

Your journey through this book

There are four Ps for raising private finance – People, Project, Paperwork, PR (or more accurately Investor Relations but that doesn't begin with a P!) – and we will look at each of these four areas in more detail.

So, one of the key areas is people. It's often said that property is a people business, so we look at the importance and the relevance of people including ourselves, and also others, and how that impacts on the whole world of raising finance.

We then look at the project, the individual properties that we're looking to finance. We look at the goals that we're trying to achieve and work out a plan to get there.

We identify that there's paperwork and legal obligations attached to all of this, and obviously making recommendations that we talk to the relevant professional people to be able to help make sure we're staying within the bounds of legality, and we look at how we can keep our investors engaged and excited by the work that we're doing.

It's about inspiring you to have the confidence to break any limiting beliefs you might have, so you understand that anybody can tap into the huge arena of private investment. There are significant amounts of money available to just be tapped into with the right proposition and the right opportunity. It is important to understand I am not giving advice on any legal aspect of raising finance or investment advice in this book, and I strongly recommend that you seek proper advice from professionals in this area.

What will you get by the end of this book?

Here's why it's worth taking the time to read this book. You're going to be inspired to take action! I include some worksheets and checklists so that you can work through as part of these to help you understand that you *can* do this and that it isn't as difficult as you might think.

The joy of this is that it will help you accelerate your journey, and the small time investment of reading this book will potentially save you years of pain and frustration because you're having to wait for investment. As soon as you understand the process and the methodology, you'll be able to tap into the massive resource that is available to you through private investor finance.

Why did I write this book?

My pleasure is derived from being able to share and help others, and this really provides me with a fantastic opportunity to give back and to help other people break through, and to teach them and to show them how to fish so that they can feed themselves rather than just giving them fish.

For me, as somebody who enjoys helping and supporting other people, that's hugely valuable. I subscribe to the idea that if you help yourself first, you're then in a much, much better place to help other people. I've been blessed with having, in some cases, traumatic learning experiences, but I choose to turn those learning experiences and research into something that is very positive and create a positive energy that can help lots of people rather than just me.

It's about helping others achieve their goals. The people I get coming into my office have such inspiring goals for what they want to achieve. I had a client who had a dream of creating social housing for victims of domestic abuse. And I just think, "Wow, if I can help them to break through to be able to do that, although I'm not directly helping the people who are victims of domestic abuse, I'm helping somebody else to do that."

Another client wanted to set up a meditation and well-being centre, again to help other people to deal with the stresses of modern life. So although I'm not actually physically doing that myself, I'm helping them to achieve that. That's a very powerful 'why' for me. It's about helping others achieve their goals and dreams, and I find that so rewarding.

I feel very blessed that I can give something back that is of value that will help not just the people that I come directly into contact with, but the people that they come into contact with as well.

When I looked on Amazon for a book like this one to help me, there was nothing out there! I realised that there was nobody else out there offering this, and I could really make a difference!

I was actually quite shocked. It's such a key area of investing in property, and yet there is absolutely nothing out there. It struck me quite forcibly that this is an area where I have gained massive amounts of experience in the last two or three years, and to be able to share that with people is fantastic. It does fill a huge gap because there aren't books out there showing people how they can raise money from private investors.

One of the comments that I get from my clients is that they feel really comfortable with my techniques because it's not the kind of double-glazing or insurance salesman type approach, so they feel they can implement it.

So this is a book for everybody who's struggled with the idea of raising finance and wants something that fits with *their* approach. We're looking at using the skills you already have, rather than creating a wham-bam generalised approach. This is about understanding people, working with people to help you achieve your goals.

There really is nothing else out there as we saw when we were doing the research for the book. It's staggering in a way that nobody's really addressed this before. I attend a huge number of property investor meetings. (I think in the last couple of years I've attended over 150 meetings, that's not counting the ones I've hosted myself or the ones that I've spoken at.) And talking to people at those meetings, it's very clear that whilst they're getting great education in terms of a particular strategy to help them to do what they want to do, most people are struggling with the idea of raising funds to help them accelerate.

That's been borne out by the huge level of interest that has been generated just in the couple of months since I've started mentioning my book and promoting the idea that it is something that people can do. It's not a black art, and you don't need to fear the process. It's something to be embraced, and I like to be able to offer help in a way that people can relate to and understand. One of the things that I do is use stories a lot to help people get the meaning of how something works and simplify what might otherwise seem like dull or boring jargon.

I'm connecting with people on a level that they can understand and relate to very easily. We're not talking jargon; we're not talking in acronyms and strange words. We're talking in a language that you use every day, that you can relate to, that means something to you and something that you can implement very quickly and very easily into your life, rather than some complex, convoluted system that involves you doing something that's maybe on the edge of being sensible or sane.

I find that people usually get to grips with this very quickly and easily because it's something that they can immediately connect with and relate to. It's not about doing something "clever" or that requires a great deal of skill in any particular area. This is something that everybody can do, everybody can understand, and everybody can implement. There's no hocus pocus. It's very simple, and it's very straightforward; I will guide you through a process that helps you understand the value in every element of it.

What is powerful is that this is accessible to everybody. It isn't just for high-flying, entrepreneurial property investors; this is for everybody from grass roots right the way through.

Why would you listen to me?

So, why me? Well, I started out my journey not having any money at all. In fact, not just having no money, I had minus money. But I didn't let that stand in my way of moving forward. My reason "why" was big enough to be able to overcome that seemingly impossible limiting factor of not having any money at all. After all, so many people tell me that they haven't got any money so they can't invest in property. I was not going to let that be a barrier to investing in property.

I hear a lot of people saying, "Well, I've run out of money," or simply "I don't have any money." But what I am saying is, "Look, you don't need to have millions in the bank in order to invest in property. With the right approach, you can attract that in."

I've raised in the region of £2.5 million in private finance in the last couple of years. If I can do it, then actually anybody can do it. There's nothing particularly special about me. I just figured out how to do it through some fairly extreme motivation from my perspective that I needed to do it.

Having done that, though, was it all a smooth journey? The answer is no, absolutely not. It was far from it, so there were lots of lessons learned on the way of things that we could have done better, things that I could improve upon and potholes and challenges that I faced along the way that are brilliant to be able to share with others. I am, therefore, well placed to identify the kinds of things that you might experience on the way and what to look out for and how to work around those.

> *"I have learned (finally) that failures and mistakes are an inherent part of success, embrace them, learn from them and take the next step. Never give up."*

I have experienced a lot of things, which certainly when you're starting out, you run the risk of experiencing if you're not prepared for them. I can help you to set yourself up, expecting some of these things to happen, rather than going blindly into a situation and finding that, "Oh my goodness, we didn't know this would happen," or, "That's caught us unawares; that leaves us exposed."

By understanding some of the things that can happen will help to give you the confidence to go out there and do it for yourself. Let's be clear, though, I don't know everything. I would never be that precocious; there is always the opportunity to learn more and to learn different ways of doing something. Who knows, it might be a better, more effective way. I try and remain open at all times in this respect.

The Blue Line

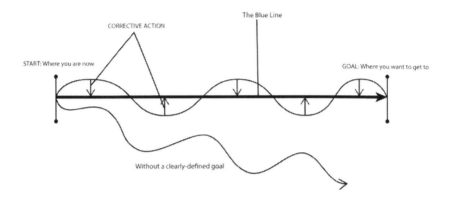

THE BLUE LINE PHILOSOPHY

I got into property a number of years ago now. When I was 50, I ran the New York Marathon, and obviously, that's a huge achievement on my part. I still remember very clearly the whole preparation, the whole day of running, and the immediate aftermath of that. I can still feel myself running up First Avenue and seeing 47,000 people ahead of me, and thinking, "That's a long way to go uphill!"

It was an extraordinary experience, but what that taught me was that if I could achieve that at the age of 50, what else could I achieve? At the time, I was involved in the horticultural world as a garden designer. I also ran a social networking site called The Garden Network. These were things that I was going to have to continue working at pretty much for the rest of my life. They certainly weren't generating any passive income that I could subsequently use for retirement.

It was brought home to me shortly after I came back from New York. I started getting involved in what I saw as opportunities at the time, but in fact, they were little more than learning experiences. I got involved with internet marketing, and all sorts of almost scam-like things that, pretty much without exception, all turned out to be too good to be true.

That exploratory time and research led me to my first property meeting. It led me to having my pension valued and establishing that actually we had a fairly major problem there because it was going to produce me less than £5,000 a year – and that was in 15 years' time – which clearly wasn't going to be enough to support my wife and four children.

So it was fairly obvious that I needed to do something more proactive towards ensuring that that figure moved from something which clearly wasn't going to be liveable on, to a level where I could choose what I did. And it's not so much about retirement, it's about the choice.

After my first property meeting, I then started exploring possibilities within property and property investment. At the time, I didn't really have any money so I was keeping my ears open for how I could work and earn money within property without having any money to start with. So I was starting from a position where I had nothing more than really an idea, and it was how that was going to work itself out. I recognised the importance of getting an education, of learning how property worked and what sort of things to look out for and how I could maximise the things that I was good at.

This led me to a Mastermind course. I did a three-day accelerator, a 12-month programme, and I went on to do a graduate programme. I was 11 months through the 12-month Mastermind programme when I realised I hadn't really done anything. I wasn't really motivated to take action because quite a lot of the strategies that were being talked about didn't resonate with me at all; they didn't excite me, and they didn't tick any boxes in terms of what I was looking for.

I was trying to replace my pension and aiming to get my time back, and I couldn't make the connection at that time between what was available and how it ticked my boxes. I could see it was working for other people, but it somehow wasn't resonating with me.

I had a two-hour crisis meeting about 11 months into the 12-month programme. At the end of it, I established that my best course of action was going to be as a connector and connecting people who had finance with people who had deals. Let's be clear though – without the Mastermind Course I wouldn't have known what was possible.

"Focus on doing things that you enjoy and are good at, you will be better than you think. Seek help for things that you don't enjoy and aren't good at, failing to do this simple thing will hold you back and drain your energy."

So I went off and started doing that, and met with great success, was mobbed by people who liked the idea of somebody else raising finance for them. To a great extent, I was very successful at doing that. But I was spending a lot of my time talking with other people and sharing my knowledge without doing it in a particularly structured way, and I certainly wasn't valuing my own time and knowledge and my experience.

It took a couple of years before I started to recognise and reflect on just how much knowledge and experience I had, and how that could potentially benefit other people. So rather than keeping it to myself, it became more and more obvious that I should actually share that.

It took somebody else to point out to me that I had that value because I didn't really believe that I was different from anybody else. I thought that everybody could do this and was, in a way, shocked to discover that I was different and that I had a different approach. It took somebody else to point that out to me rather than me recognising it myself. Now it's been pointed out, it's blindingly obvious, and I'm kind of kicking myself for not recognising it myself. But actually, the reality is I wasn't ready then to share my knowledge and experience because of where I was on a personal level.

So it's needed that journey, and for me to go through some challenging experiences, to get myself into a place where I can now step back, reflect, and then share my knowledge with people in a meaningful way.

Why I'm excited for you

This is likely to be breakthrough territory for most people. Whilst I understand there are some people who are happy and comfortable working with private investors, there is a huge percentage of people for whom this is really challenging. What's so exciting is that because we've systemised it and because we've taken time and trouble to make this understandable and easy to follow, a very straightforward process, it makes it accessible to everybody. This breaks down the myths and the barriers that people perceive are there.

So it opens up a huge world of possibilities because if you've got access to potentially unlimited finance, it allows you to set bigger, more ambitious goals to achieve, and you needn't be restricted by things that have been holding you back. So that's just awesome from my perspective, to be able to help you to make changes and to understand that you can do it. This book contains the tools to help propel you forward and achieve your goals.

Once you master these skills, there's nothing that can't be achieved. It's something that's going to be with you for the rest of your life. Once you understand the mechanics of this, the mechanics aren't going to change. The rules and regulations may change, but it's not the critical aspect of it. The critical aspect of it is understanding what pain points you're addressing, how you're providing a solution for those people and how you're able to help everybody all the way through.

One small change can make all the difference

I was talking with one of my clients about the value of changing the way that you do things, and he came out with this great story. He was an officer in the navy and shared a story about how closely they need to shave in the navy. He shaved about three times over, and it gave him a really painful shaving rash. When he left the navy, he was still continuing to shave in the way that he had to shave while he was in the navy, and he was still suffering from the rash. One day, he decided that in order to get rid of the rash, he had to do something different. Because carrying on doing the same thing each morning wasn't going to change the situation, so he modified the way he shaved. The rash then subsided, and now he's rash free, just because he changed the way that he did it.

I think there's a really important lesson there – that if we carry on doing the same thing, time and time again and expect things to change, it's just not going to happen. Even if it's a relatively small change in direction, it can have a massive impact. I know from my own personal experience, I spent a lot of time working from home and had a small room in the back of the house where I hid myself away. It became very, very claustrophobic – it was cramped, cluttered and not conducive to a proper working environment, and it actually took somebody else to point out that changing that environment was probably the only way of breaking out of the kind of routine and negative connotations of always tripping over myself and hunting for things because it just wasn't the space to lay things out and to have clarity. I took a very big leap of sourcing some office space, and the difference that made within about a week was astonishing. It changed my perception of what I was doing; it changed the space and the organization that I had and more or less immediately started attracting more high-quality clients into that environment. Just being open to that change process is extraordinary.

We all get comfortable with what we're doing, and it's sometimes easy to just keep going. I think there's an expression, "Better the devil you know." We get very comfortable in our daily routines and the things we do repetitively without really questioning why we're doing them or the benefit it's bringing us to do them in a particular way. Sometimes even a small change can have a dramatic effect on the outcome.

MINDSET AND SETTING GOALS

Is it easy to find money to buy property?

The fear I think everybody has with finding money is that money is scarce and will, therefore, be a problem to find any. One of the limiting beliefs that many people have is that money is hard to come by, and I think it's a common misconception that it's going to be hard, it's going to be difficult, and so there's immediately a barrier, a blocker up there. Conversely, if you talk to people who are involved in money and finance, you'll understand that money is everywhere, and it flows, and it's simply a case of getting into that flow to be able to access it. So, the common perception is that money is scarce; however, the reverse is true.

Often an area that we are not familiar with can seem overwhelming and out of reach. We see our own lack of finance reflected in how we perceive the world around us. Changing your perspective will help you be open.

What if I need to find money in a hurry?

Finding money in a hurry; it's one of those situations that I encountered when all my existing contacts had been approached previously and had all come back with a fairly resounding 'no', or they had actually pledged money for an assortment of other projects. I had one of those terrible phone calls on a Tuesday lunchtime, and you know that when the call was coming in that there's going to be a bad message in there, and the voice at the other end of the phone said, "Tim, we need you to work your magic. We need £150,000 by Friday."

Now, having already been to all of my contacts, I'd got to where we'd exhausted every possibility, or at least I thought we had, my response to the question wasn't that we can't do this, but simply, "Okay, what's the bank account number that we need to put that money into?" Because I knew that with the right approach it would be possible to find that money and we would get that money in.

I'm not saying it's easy, and I wouldn't necessarily recommend it because the stress levels do go up, but it is possible to do. The money is out there, and it's possible to access it with the right approach, and the key is just getting that approach right.

Case Study 2

We were looking to finance an HMO in Swindon. The figures for buying and refurbing it all stacked up, and we had a team of people there, so we had somebody who had his own building team ready to go and actually developed the property once we got it there. We'd set our budget very carefully so that we knew that we needed £50,000 in order to purchase and do the necessary work.

It was possible at that time to get a mortgage and also get the development finance separately, so we knew that we needed £50,000 in total to complete the project. There was also the possibility of getting planning permission at the bottom of the garden to put in a further property. So we were looking at adding value in a number of different ways, both to the property that existed, and also potential within the garden.

This one would have been fantastic, but we had our investor pull out at 9 p.m. the evening before we were due to exchange at 12 noon the following day, highlighting the need for a back-up plan when you've got investors. Just because they say they've got cash available doesn't necessarily mean it's going to be forthcoming.

So that was quite a harsh learning experience because we then had to explain to the estate agent that we weren't able to proceed despite what we'd told them the day before, because we didn't have money in our bank account, it was still sitting in our investor's bank account, for reasons personal to him. He wasn't able to release it because he had a change of circumstances; we couldn't blame him for that, but it did leave us exposed.

I think that was a really good learning experience: we'd done all the due diligence, everybody was happy to go ahead, we were comfortable that the property was a really good deal and that there was plenty of development opportunity available in it, but we missed it because we hadn't been diligent enough in terms of finding alternative options on the finance.

Looking back, my recommendations would be that when you're looking at investor finance, that if somebody says they've got money available, just be clear about when it's available and assess whether actually it's worth getting the money in the bank sooner rather than later.

Each situation will be different obviously, but in some instances, it's worth actually getting control of the money and making sure that it's worth paying a premium in terms of the interest. Sometimes, even though you might not be ready to go with the project, just secure the finance as soon as you can. Obviously, each project is individual, and each circumstance is specific to an individual, so you don't know necessarily what's going to work in each case but just be aware that just because an investor says, "Yes, I'm interested, and I've got the money available," until you've physically got the cash in your bank, it doesn't follow that it's available for you. So have a back-up plan in place.

Why raising money is like catching butterflies

You need to shift your thinking from asking to attracting. One of the analogies that I use to help demonstrate to people how to attract finance is that of attracting butterflies. I think this is an important thing to stress here: we are attracting money; we're not begging for it, we're not desperate, and we aren't trying to sell anything. It's about presenting an opportunity to the right person at the right time, and the way that I illustrate this is by sharing a story that there are a number of different ways to catch a butterfly.

You can stand in your garden with a butterfly net and wait, and you can wait for that butterfly to fly by, and when it does fly by, you can run around the garden and chase it with your net and hope that you can catch it. But it's a very random process. You're reliant on a butterfly coming over your garden and being able to chase it. You don't have any say as to what kind of butterfly that is, and it may not be the butterfly that you want.

By contrast, taking ourselves back into the garden again, if we wanted to attract, let's say, a cabbage white into the garden, a really good plant to grow would be a cabbage because cabbage whites will come flocking to lay their eggs, and you'll have a proliferation of cabbage white butterflies. You won't be able to keep them out of the garden. That's great if you want cabbage whites.

If you want Painted Lady or Red Admiral butterflies or something a little bit more exotic, a bit higher value shall we say, you'd be better off planting something like a buddleia, which is known as the butterfly bush, which has lovely purple flowers that will attract more vibrant types of butterfly than the common cabbage white.

The analogy here is that by creating the right garden or the right atmosphere, the right scenario for the right type of investor, you will attract them in. The whole point here is that by understanding who your ideal investor is, and what kind of project they might be interested in, it will help you then to create the garden and present the project in such a way that you will get the right kind of person. And rather than waiting for them to come flying by, you'll be attracting them in. So many people get this wrong and end up chasing investors away rather than bringing them onboard. This leads to frustration and reinforces the myth that it's difficult to raise private finance.

By having the right message for the right type of person, you are attracting these people into your garden. The relevance of that is by understanding what is important to those investors, you will create something that appeals to them, addresses their pain, and they will want to find out more. They'll want to get involved because it's something you've attracted them to.

So, it's breaking down that limiting belief that most people who are seeking private finance have which is that they are begging for money or asking for money. It's not a terribly British sort of thing to do, to go around asking people for money or even talking about it. People don't even like talking about money.

So, the butterfly in the garden analysis I hope is a clear indication as to how you can create something that is appealing and attractive that will draw people into your opportunity. It is just that, it's an opportunity. You understand what their pain point is, and we need to go back perhaps to look at what the pain of an investor might be. What do you think that pain might be? What is their frustration or blocker? Typically, the pain point that is experienced from investors is that we've experienced, in this country, historically low interest rates for many years.

Savers, who've got money perhaps in a bank or a building society, are getting a really tragically low amount of return for the money sitting in the bank. By the time you've taken inflation into account, we've got a situation where actually they're probably losing money, not making it.

So, I think it's important here not to pre-judge people.

Quite often I get people saying to me, "Well, I don't know anybody who's got money." It's that same Britishness: we don't talk about the money that we do have. So just turn that on its head. Just because people aren't talking about the fact that they've got money, and people won't talk about that, doesn't mean to say that they haven't got it. Why would you broadcast this fact? I know people who own flash cars and live in expensive, desirable property that don't necessarily have any money! They have spent most of it acquiring toys and playthings rather than investing. Of course, these people may have investment money, but don't be fooled by the exterior.

So who has this kind of money, and who are these people?

One of the first questions that people ask me is: "Who's got this money?" I think it's a broader spectrum of people than you might expect, and there's no reason actually why pretty much everybody might not have some money stashed away in some sort of savings account. It might be in a pension account, and the changes in pension regulations mean that there is more pension funding available currently, and people are looking at what they can do with their pension pots to get a better return than they're getting at the moment. There are all types of investment tools now available for pensions; SIPP's are probably the best known, but SSAS schemes are gaining in popularity. I'm not a pensions adviser, but I strongly suggest you talk to someone who is and get proper professional advice. If you want to talk to me about my SSAS, do get in touch, happy to discuss why I chose what I did.

So, don't be restricted in ... just because people don't outwardly show that they've got cash available, they might be the ones sitting on a quiet little hoard. They may have inherited it; in some instances, they may have won it, but it's possible that it's their life savings. It's possible it's come from pension pots. There is a lot of money in, shall we say, the system, and it is a case of tapping into that resource and understanding how to access it.

Be aware also that there are vehicles like the SEIS and EIS schemes that can be used for accessing funds. Talk to your property tax specialist about accessing this type of funding and learn what the benefits are to investors. The method you use to attract them will still be the same as for attracting other investors.

You have also got a proliferation of crowd funding platforms available now, a few of which will support property projects. There are specialist property based platforms out there which can be used for funding. Do make sure you have a suitable exit strategy lined up for when the crowd needs repaying. Again the same rules apply.

Why your perception of people who have money, or investors, may be completely wrong.

I think the perception is that people should be perhaps exhibiting what are perceived as signs of wealth. I think it's quite important not to do that.

So, you're not prejudging anybody in terms of what they may or may not have. Very often, they don't display outwardly signs of what people might perceive wealth to be: maybe that's a big house or a big car or expensive holidays and all those sorts of things. Quite frequently, it's the people who don't live in a big house, who don't drive a flash car, who don't go on expensive holidays, who are actually the frugal ones who have saved, in some cases, quite considerable pots but don't necessarily strut around like a peacock displaying that wealth. They may be more cautious in their approach.

So, the message here is, don't pre-judge anybody just because they don't appear, in your eyes to have that cash readily available, as it were.

Why £200,000 investment may be easier to find than you think ...

I've had a number of investors where externally they don't display any sort of what might be regarded as signs of wealth, but inwardly, they've perhaps got £100,000, maybe £200,000, sitting available. For example, a lady who I only met very, very briefly once, who was a connection on LinkedIn, was a pharmacy manager, and she had £200,000 ready to invest.

So, would I have associated a pharmacy manager with having that sort of money available? No, absolutely not. But she did.

I've also come across somebody who was a pensioner who lived in a very modest house, had aspirations to grow his funds, and he handed over £100,000 almost without thinking about it. Clearly, I presented a case that outlined the details of the project and the risks attached, but the point is the cash is out there waiting for you. Obviously, I've disguised people's identities to protect their privacy.

THE FIRST STEPS TO TAKE

So you need to find money for a property. Here are the first steps that you need to take ...

The first thing to do is to understand the value that you bring. One of the exercises that I get my clients to do is what we call *The 30 Unique Things About You*. This is not just a list, it's understanding why people would come to you. What do they come to you for? What attracts people?

Thirty things that are Unique about me and why people come to me

1. Great connector
2. Superb supporter
3. Motivator
4. Action taker
5. Perseveres
6. Resourceful
7. Intelligent
8. Communicator
9. Friendly
10. Flexible
11. Accelerator
12. Good listener
13. Articulate
14. Sociable
15. Open minded
16. Experienced
17. Honest
18. Humble

19. Confident
20. Cheerful
21. Fun loving
22. Exploring
23. Passionate
24. Big picture thinker
25. Large network of great contacts
26. Simplifier
27. Hard worker
28. Team player
29. Leader
30. Knowledgeable

So, it's kind of merging in with the butterfly thing, but taking a look at yourself first and why people would come to you. What specialist skills that you maybe have, or what competencies? What would attract people to you as a person? What makes you different from everybody else in the world? It's important to understand that we are all different and that we do have differences and that those are to be celebrated and not to be diminished or hidden away from.

Those differences are critical because property is a people business, and we're presenting ourselves as a person that somebody else would trust and like and want to work with. So, understanding why people would come to you is really important. It's, if you like, painting your feathers so that you're attracting the right people in by understanding who you are.

"Know where you are starting and have a definite, clear goal to work towards. Tell everyone where you are going, when you give others clarity they will know how to support you."

As part of working with me, it's a great idea to write it down, and keep that list to hand so that you can add things that maybe your friends or family comment or contribute to that list. So it's a living list, just giving you confidence in yourself to understand that you add value and how you do that.

What if you don't feel that you're important enough or have the experience to do this?

Firstly, you are not alone. This is a common problem faced by many would be investors. This is why I encourage you to write a list of at least 30 things that are unique and different about you. Really dig deep into that, and if you have trouble doing that, approach family and friends to get their input and help you on your way. Choose people who know you well.

It's unique qualities that differentiate you from everybody else on the planet. So, what I mean by that is not that you've got two dogs but that you're maybe a caring person, that you're enthusiastic, that you're maybe good with numbers, good with people, have a drive and dedication, so those are the sorts of qualities that we're looking for. These are things that would attract other people to you.

You're really just trying to dig deep into what are the things that draw people to you. If you were a plant, and you were a cabbage, you'd be attracting cabbage whites. So, what is it about the cabbage that attracts cabbage whites? Don't think for one moment I think you are a cabbage! But I'll wager that you are having those sorts of thoughts and that you are in some way not good enough to do this. Time for a little dose of self-belief!

Okay, so I've got my list of 30 unique things about me, what's my next step?

Your next step is to understand the type of person that might be attracted by those qualities. So, who would find those qualities attractive?

Property's all about people. There is an element of the project and various other elements as well, so it's primarily about people. So, it's understanding the kind of person that would want to be associated with you.

I'll give you an example. I'm, generally speaking, quite a people-related person, but I'm not terribly good at doing detail and systems and numbers and that sort of thing. So just understanding how I would need to approach somebody like that, it's important to know what somebody is going to be looking for from you. Even if it is not a strength, you still need to be able to accommodate the requirements of your investor. You might need to look at your team for support in a particular area to ensure all bases are covered. Remember, no one expects you to be able to do everything yourself.

What are the qualities that make you trustworthy to different investors?

One example I use is, if somebody wanted to raise £5 million for a property project, they'd be talking to a different kind of person to somebody who wanted to raise £50,000. The profile of the person they were talking to would be very different.

They'd probably have a different attitude to money as a value. They may have a different attitude to risk. They may have a different attitude towards the level of detail that they would want to see in order to make a decision about investing in a project. They may want to know more about the project team that was involved in it, levels of experience. And different people will want different things from you, depending on how they view property, where they're getting their information from, what their knowledge is about property as an investment. They will have a pre-formed idea about the levels of risk and, therefore, the type of person. If you've got something that's a very risky project, talking to somebody who is risk-averse isn't going to get you the finance.

So, understanding where people sit and who you are looking to attract in will help you approach those people, and when you are talking to them, you'll be able to sift through the people who are likely to be interested against those who are never going to be.

Where exactly will I go to find people like this?

As I mentioned earlier in this book, investors are everywhere. They don't necessarily wear big rosettes to say, "I'm an investor, I'm holding a flag up to say, *Look I'm an investor!*"

I think this is important when you are approaching investors. The approach is not direct, it's more indirect. And because investors potentially are everywhere, we look at leveraging the people that we know to access their networks as well.

For example, we might only have a network of, let's say, 100 people, and we might say that's not very many people to approach, and I would be inclined to agree. However, if we prepare our presentation to those 100 people in such a way that we're accessing or potentially have access to all of their contacts as well, and let's say they will have 100 contacts each, and in this day of social networking and online connectivity, 100 contacts is a really low number. Actually, by the time we've multiplied that up, we've got 100 times 100, which means 10,000 people that we potentially have access to, if we get our message right.

It comes back to this: we're not begging; we're presenting an opportunity. If you present it in such a way that it might appeal to both people that you are approaching directly, but might also stimulate them to contact people perhaps while they're sitting around at a dinner party or having a drink in the pub, or at a social networking meeting, whatever it might be, you're getting much more traction than by simply looking at the people who are perhaps facing you directly. This leverage will dramatically improve your chances of raising finance more effectively.

These people might be family, they might be friends, they might be networking contacts, or they might be people that you're connected to on Facebook. LinkedIn, for example, is a fabulous platform for making these sorts of connections. Also, going out to networking meetings, not necessarily property investing networking meetings, but breakfast, lunch, and evening meetings, places where people meet and you can exchange ideas.

When you are looking for potential groups that you might tap into, think back to your list of the 30 things that make you unique. Do you have any particular areas of interest, a sport perhaps, sailing, golf, rugby or another interest such as wine, music, walking? Are there local groups that you might join to meet up with others on an informal basis? How might you use this to your advantage? If there isn't a specific group locally that fits the bill, how about setting up your own group? If, for example, your passion is wine, might it be possible to create a group that combined your love of wine with property and investing? You might need to experiment with formats to find a formula that works, but by creating a group, you will be seen as the 'go to' person. You are presenting yourself to others in a favourable light and building relationships and trust.

Case Study 3

My client Grantley was just starting out, and his biggest problem was lack of focus. He was trying to do too many things in too little time. In the first session, we got him to narrow down his thinking so that he was much more clearly focused on one thing rather than 30 things. He estimated that in that one session, we saved him about eight months' time of messing around and going the wrong way and not really achieving anything.

That really just shows the importance of being clear about what your goal is, what you want to achieve, because you can then set out a very clear path to achieving that. It's much easier if you know where you're going, to set clear action points to tick off as you go. If you don't know where you're going, you can't do that. I forget who it was that said, "Taking action on things that were never necessary is the biggest waste of time and energy that you can expend." If there's no point in doing something, why are you spending time doing it?

We saw this very clearly. He was taking lots of action, but it was to what purpose, to what goal? What was it actually achieving? He couldn't answer those questions, so it helped to bring clarity to the situation and allowed him to focus more clearly on what he was doing. He could then articulate that more clearly with the people he had around him, so they had a better idea of what he was doing, and what his aims were, and were better able then to support him and guide him and work with him to achieve his goals.

So it had a combined snowball effect if you like, of bringing greater clarity to the whole process, not just the front end of it, which has ultimately impacted in being able to go on and take more action in other areas that still support his goals.

The benefits of meeting the right person in the right place at the right time

Networking gives you other enormous benefits as well as the straightforward raising of finance. Another benefit is sharing what you are doing with other people and then discovering the synergy between what you're doing and what the other person is doing. For example, recently, I've met with people who have added massive value to what I'm doing, just by me sharing with them what I'm doing. They see it from a different perspective, which is refreshing and helpful. The key to this is to present yourself in a way that is not a know-it-all way as if you're big and brash and kind of strutting around, like you're not open to ideas and not open to receiving.

An interesting challenge, as somebody who is used to giving a lot, is that it took me quite a while to understand that in order to give, somebody has to receive. In fact, *not* receiving is denying somebody else the opportunity to give. I think once I realised this and became more open to seeing where others were trying to give and paid attention to and listened to that, all of a sudden people started sharing their experience and expertise.

For example, Mark is a qualified accountant, has had a practice for 15 years, and he's a serial entrepreneur. He's experienced in all sorts of different disciplines, and because of all that experience, he can take a look at what I'm doing and see it from an entirely different perspective, and see opportunities that I wouldn't have even known existed. In a way, it was almost too much, and I had to hold him back because he was starting to take me into overwhelm just in the half hour meeting that we had. I recognised there was huge value there, so I arranged to spend more time with him and drill down into a couple of specific areas to get comfortable with those before exploring some of the other things that might be possible as well. Just that half hour meeting I had will potentially generate tens of thousands of pounds worth of revenue in the coming years. It's that massive. Just by being open, being receptive to the other person. It is also important to be open to that, to be gracious, and to recognise the value. Now, is that going to happen at every meeting with every person? No, but don't let that deter you from exploring!

Another example: I met up with somebody recently that I've known for four years, and we were due to have an hour's meeting. It was such a beautiful setting; we were sitting at a beach front cafe, beautiful clear skies, boats sailing past in the bay, and we had our first hour's meeting, but it was so nice we had another coffee to see what else we could talk about. In fact, we kept going for three hours, and interestingly, the most productive, most rewarding ideas came in that third hour when we were completely relaxed. We were both very open to receiving what the other was giving, and it was a very spacious place we were in; we weren't enclosed in an office. Overlooking the ocean on a clear sunny day, the environment was different from normal, and that had quite an impact. In fact, the chap that I was meeting with commented that quite frequently his best ideas came when they shut the doors to the office and went for a walk; it just allowed the space and the clarity to fall into place, and that can be very powerful. We discussed possible joint ventures, opportunities for working together using our respective skill sets. We discussed the framework for how working together might be beneficial and the values that mattered to each of us. Never underestimate the value of spending time to build relationships ahead of doing business together.

The value that you get from networking is not just about money, it's about contacts, information. It's learning about tax opportunities relevant to your personal situation; it's a whole range of things. It's about filling in a bigger picture and not being blinded by the moment. Be open to the opportunities. Listen to what is being said by others when you are in the room, and above all, follow up. So often I see situations where it is clear that people aren't really listening to what is being said.

Frequently at networking events, you get an opportunity to deliver an elevator pitch about what you do or what you are looking for. Listen and make notes about who is standing up. These people may not be of immediate interest to you but noticing who they are and connecting with them to find out more will stand you in good stead. Often, I get people at these meetings asking me after everyone has had their chance of speaking, things like is there anyone locally who sources deals? There may have been two or three people who just stood up and said that is exactly what they do, yet they missed it.

Whilst this continues to baffle me, it does present you with an opportunity. If everyone else is missing opportunities and you start to pick up on them, do you think you might give yourself a huge advantage? I take a small notebook to each meeting to jot down details of everyone I meet. Then I make sure I follow up with each person with a reminder about the meeting and asking if there is anything I can do to help them in any way.

How to network successfully ...

This could easily be the topic for a whole book. There are definite skills involved in networking successfully, but here are some basic guidelines to help you get started. You could arrange to go to business networking meetings, to social groups or a sports club. My main recommendation would be to attend networking meetings. Generally speaking, people who are going to networking meetings of any sort are going there for a purpose, and that's to further their own network, to build their network, to build contacts, and quite a few of the business networks work on a referral basis, so they are looking to refer people.

So, I understand that networking isn't necessarily everybody's cup of tea, and there are some fairly simple things that you can do at a network meeting. For me, personally, I quite enjoy going in and saying hello to everybody in the room. I recognise that's not in everybody's comfort zone, but even if you talk to two or three people, go to a networking meeting and make a specific effort to make contact with two or three people. Remember, it is not just the person you are connecting with, it is accessing their own network to leverage that effectively too. So for every person that you connect with effectively, you are potentially adding hundreds if not thousands of extra potential. That puts a very different spin on things!

How to network like a pro

When you arrive at a business meeting, there may sometimes be 100 people in the room. How do you decide who to talk to? Do you research them first? Do you have a checklist of key people to talk to?

It depends a little bit on the meeting that I'm going to. If I know who is going to be there, then I'll make a specific effort to go and talk to certain key people. Perhaps I'll have an agenda that I want to look at and address with them.

However, for most meetings, I don't go with that sort of agenda. I go there and, on the way while I'm driving or on the train, I'll be imagining what it is that I'm going there for. So, I go with a purpose, not just pitching up at the meeting to say "hi" to people. I've got a purpose, a very specific purpose when I go to a meeting. Depending on what that meeting is will depend on what the desired outcomes from that meeting are. It's the same with anything: it's setting that goal and defining it clearly so that your brain knows that it has to execute that.

So, for example, going to a property meeting I will be looking to come away with at least five new contacts from that meeting. So, that's five people that I've never spoken to before at the meeting, that I don't really know anything about, and I will be looking to add them to my list of contacts. But it will be with a very specific goal in mind. So, if I'm specifically looking for investment finance, I will steer the conversation towards what I'm looking for, and the whole time I'll be asking questions that will be not direct questions, but perhaps indirect questions aimed at establishing why the other person is at the meeting, what their particular challenges are that they're facing at the moment, what issues they are facing. If they could get help, what would that look like to them? And I show an interest in them – I'm interested in where they are in their journey. Are they just starting out, or are they a long way down the line? for example.

If I'm going to a more general business meeting, I might be inquiring as to what challenges they were facing in their business world; is there a way that I can add value through some of the other people I've met in connecting them together? Sometimes it might be something that's quite obscure, but it's just picking up something that allows you to get an extra hook into the business of actually generating communication between two parties. So, in the same way, I enjoy sailing, so if someone else is interested in sailing, then I've immediately got something other than property that we can talk about; it's an extra way of engaging with them, rather than just having to focus on one subject all the time. It just helps to break up a meeting or a discussion. It's about asking people questions, and that's one of the key things really.

For me, personally, I have trouble hearing, so I find it difficult to be in a large group. I like to talk to people on a more one-to-one basis. So, I prefer to focus on one person at the time, rather than big groups. I find that easier for me personally to deal with than a larger group – partially because I have hearing difficulties -– I'll be looking to try to engage with somebody on a one-to-one basis rather than as a group discussion. Because it's easier then to ask individual questions to that one person rather than trying to ask general questions to a group.

How to break the ice with strangers …

I've been to a lot of meetings, probably over 150 of them – that's excluding the ones I've hosted, and I've spoken at.

I did not really know anybody in the room when I arrived, and that can be quite daunting even for someone like me who is good at talking to people.

What I do in that situation, rather than talk to many people, I single out people who are maybe on their own or look like they are not uncomfortable in the room. Rather than going to join a group of people who know each other, I go and find people who are perhaps sitting or standing on their own. I just try to break the ice with very simple questions like, "Is this your regular meeting?" or the classic, "Do you come here often?"

You are trying to establish if this is perhaps their local area. Are they new to property investing? Do they have any properties?

This is not going to be a long conversation necessarily with somebody because if you travelled a long way, like an hour and a half, to get to the meeting, you would want to meet as many people in the room as you can.

If you are less comfortable with meeting with the whole room, then you will find it is more comfortable meeting two or three people. That is fine, providing you get value out of it – so you are looking to ask them questions and to engage with them. The kind of questions that break the ice are the classics, and not especially original, such as "Do you come here often?" and "Is it a regular meeting?"

What to ask to break the ice

- Are you already an investor?
- Are you investing currently?
- Are you just starting out?
- Have you ever had any property training or education?
- What brings you to this meeting?
- What particular challenges are you facing at present?

So you're building a picture of where they are with their training. Then you can move on to the next step and ask questions like, "What are the major challenges that you're facing at the moment?" and "What are the blockers you are experiencing at the moment?"

It might be they have trouble finding property, or they're having trouble finding bank or building society accounts that pay decent interest, or they have got money but don't have time. People will start to open up if you start asking them questions.

If you come in and start talking about yourself all the time, you are never going to find anything out about the other person.

The goal is to find out about them and to be interested in the other person.

It does not matter what you do at all. It is about finding out what makes the other person tick. The more questions you can go armed with, the better. It does not matter if it is a property meeting or business meeting, a private party or a gathering at a sports event, but use some simple, non-threatening, non-aggressive questions that are inquiring as to where somebody is.

It might be that an element of subtlety or discretion is required. You may have to park the conversation for a while, to make a mental or physical note in a notebook to come back to it because some people may not be ready for you right now, and that is fine. It is about building a relationship and building rapport. Very often, people will indicate they are not ready because of where they happen to be in their journey. Think of it as an exploration. Do they perhaps know other people who might be a good fit? So, who else do they know? Do they have friends that come to the meeting or do not come to the meeting?

It is about asking intelligent questions.

Networking isn't like speed dating

Some people treat networking like speed dating type, trying to get around 25 people or more in one evening. I am not a big fan of this. It is one of the biggest errors that people make. They come blasting in the room; they come armed with 50 business cards. They are determined, at all cost, to make sure everyone in the room has a copy of their card, and the end of the evening, you frequently find all of those cards either on the floor or the bin because people did not have the opportunity to engage with them, so actually that approach can be counterproductive.

If you are a competent and confident networker, it is possible to get around many people. I would recommend, particularly when you are starting, if you are not a confident networker, to focus on setting a target when you go to meetings.

You can meet people an hour or so before the meeting. There is usually a ten-minute networking break in the middle, and there is the end of the evening.

In the worst case, you might come came away with three new contacts; people you have not spoken to before. So aim for one person before the meeting, one person during the break, and one afterwards. If you are somebody who is not a confident networker, just come away with that.

It is possible to do quite a lot more than when you are more experienced, but even if you come away with just three from each meeting, and you've engaged with them properly, you will start to build your network. The important thing is you cannot expect to go to just one network meeting and think, "That is it. I'm done now."

This is about building a relationship, about building trust, so the next time you go to the meeting, you might find the same three people there that you engaged with last time. You can exchange pleasantries such as "How you are getting on? Did you manage to overcome to problem you mentioned last time?"

Then park that fairly quickly before moving on to somebody else you've not engaged with previously, to carry on networking.

It is all about asking questions and engaging. It is about asking questions and listening to the responses.

Why networking is like courting

The big mistake that people make is they go along to a networking meeting, say, "Hi, my name's Tim," and the next question is, "Would you like to invest £50,000 in a property project?" Now, that's a little bit like going to a party and marching in and saying to the first girl that you meet, having just stepped over the door, "Hi, my name's Tim, would you like to marry me?"

But that's how people do it. Personally, I've had something literally overnight where somebody's connected with me on LinkedIn, and they've said, "Hi, my name is X, are you interested in investing?" to which I've responded, "Possibly," and I've been bombarded with sales messages.

They have no idea what I'm looking for. There's no time or trouble being made to get to know who I am or what might be of interest to me. So they've kind of missed out the whole courting process. I think because of social media, we've forgotten the art of just simple rapport-building. It's about asking questions of the other person to understand more about what makes them tick.

I forget who said it, but to be *interesting*, you need to be *interested*. So, by asking questions of the other person, you're actually appearing interesting to them, because they're talking about the one thing that they really, really want to talk about, which is themselves.

So, networking is about going and asking people questions, but it's not about blabbing about yourself at all. It's about asking questions of the other people. It's something that you need to do, and whether you're doing it online or offline, the same rules apply. You don't go to a party and ask the first girl that you meet to jump into bed with you.

It's common sense. But, as I've discovered quite a lot, common sense is surprisingly uncommon. People, because there's a fear factor, a limiting belief that they've got, they've forgotten this art of building rapport. If you think back to the friends that you've got, you didn't suddenly become best friends the first time you met somebody.

There are cases where people talk about love at first sight, but generally speaking, a friendship and a relationship builds over time. It's not the result of a two-second conversation; it's built up over time. And yes, it's possible to raise finance really, really quickly from people you don't know, but I wouldn't recommend it. It's hard work, it's challenging, and certainly not when you're starting out; it's about building relationships, about showing interest in what other people do, understanding what pain and what problems they're experiencing by asking questions and listening to what their response is.

Once you've built that trust, then you can start sharing with them what you're doing. What kind of projects you're involved in, because if you've shown an interest in them, they are then more likely to be interested in finding out more about you. Because by being interested in what they're doing, you come across, and you portray yourself as being interesting, and therefore, people are likely to trust you more as a kickback from that.

Work on building rapport

Some people can build rapport really, really quickly, whereas other people need time to build that relationship. Everybody is different. You've identified 30 things that make you unique, and everybody that you talk to is going to have 30 or more things that make them unique.

So, there's never going to be a situation where two people follow exactly the same path. Different people will respond in different ways, and you can't necessarily gauge that. Again, it comes back to asking the questions and feeling your way a little bit. But you will start to get to a point where people will start to ask questions of you about what it is that you're doing.

Again, rather than ramming stuff down their throats, you almost need to counter that with more questions, rather than by forcing stuff onto them. That's one of the key things where people tend to fall over themselves. To use maybe a fishing analogy, they've gone out, they've cast their line, they've got a bit of a nibble, and they've started reeling in before the fish is actually on the hook. They've missed out maybe a few stages, and they haven't taken the time to really dig deep and understand what is really motivating them. It's quite hard then to go back because you've broken that trust.

So, the emphasis the whole time is on asking questions and understanding when you've got it right.

Not-working

At a meeting recently, I observed two people who were trying to network, but it clearly was *not*-working rather than *networking.* There were two people – one was a commercial finance broker who went around butting into people's conversations, handing out his business cards. He was telling people that he could help them, without even stopping to find out what they were interested in or what their challenges were, what their problems might have been. I observed him from a distance, and I think he would've struggled that night – he was clearly pushing at people, and I don't suppose for a minute many people will actually follow up on it because he was too interested in himself.

There was somebody else in the room, a lady, who had a handful of leaflets promoting a charity bike ride or something like that. She wasn't engaging with anybody; she was just roaming the room. As one of the helpers at that event, I spent 20 minutes at the end of the meeting cleaning up all of her leaflets that had just been left on the chairs and on the floor. She would have done much better to stop and engage with people to find out if they were interested in riding bikes, rather than bothering people with all these little notices. With a little careful planning, had she approached a few people and engaged with them, asking questions about why they were attending the meeting and sharing a little of her story, her 'why' she was involved with the charity event, she might have had rather more success. Each person that she actually connected with might have had family or friends who might have been interested in doing it together, as it was, take up was clearly very low.

We hadn't seen her before that particular meeting; we had no idea who she was, where she'd come from, what she was doing. What a waste of money and time – because every single one of the leaflets must have been left. There wasn't a chair that didn't have one on it, and there were a number on the floor. She hadn't achieved anything. She would have done better if she had spoken with one person and got engagement than to have wasted the entire evening achieving nothing.

Getting out of your own way

If you are going into a networking meeting, you have to understand why everybody is there. They are all there to engage, to talk, to make contact.

Most networking meetings that I have been to, you usually have some sort of badge or name identifier so you know who people are. It is OK simply going up to people to say, "Hello." I understand some people are less confident about that, but if you are serious about raising finance and doing property, you have to face your fears and kind of get over yourself in a way.

If you are getting in your own way, then it is a problem. You have to identify the things that are getting in your way. Frequently, people often do have limiting beliefs, and what I do is help people to overcome that.

If you identify those things, then you can work out 'why'. If your goal is clear enough, it will give you the motivation to achieve the goal you want.

Your 'why' has to be bigger than your fears. Fear is an acronym for "false expectations appearing real" or "future expectations appearing real". In other words: something in future that we do not necessarily have control over kind of consumes us and gets in the way of us taking action.

The best thing to do if you've got fears like that is to write them down, and if you've got a coach, a mentor, or a friend, then ask them to help you look at how you might overcome those issues.

It all boils down to: do you want this or don't you want this? If you do want to do it, you have to get over yourself. Do whatever it takes to break down those barriers. You don't necessarily have to go over the wall, but who said you cannot go around it? Find a way to be able to do it.

I did a Property Mastermind years ago, and I recall in our monthly workshop, we had a session where the task for that day was to ring up an estate agent. The person I buddied up with was literally in tears. She was trembling; terrified would be the word, at the prospect of speaking to another person at the end of the phone.

Being a caring supporter by nature, I said, "OK, rather than you do this, why don't you come sit with me while I do it?" And she did.

In fact, having someone there in that state while I was trying to make the calls was actually bewildering for me as well. It was having an impact on me. This made me feel like: "If someone is this shaken up, then maybe there is something here to be afraid of. Maybe I am not fine either. Maybe there is something wrong with me, and maybe I should be terrified. Maybe I should be in pieces."

This kind of talk goes into your mind and takes over, and I get that because I have had those kinds of experiences myself in the past. There are times when I cannot pick up the phone or I cannot face meeting up with somebody maybe because I am having a bad day.

But happily, this particular person recognised her own limiting factor and limiting belief. So she decided in order to overcome it that she would get a job with somebody in the property world who was very experienced. Her job was to make telephone calls to the landlords, so she had to "eat that frog" as

Brian Tracy would say.

She was confronted with a box load of frogs in the morning, and she did this one or two days a week for three or four months. Her job was to try to secure purchase lease options, which is not easy, but she went into an environment where other people were making those calls as well. So she had the support from somebody who was guiding her about what to say and how to say it, how to do it.

She now owns a very, very profitable property business because she has faced and confronted her fears. She is not a natural networker, but she knows when she has broken the ice; she is comfortable with talking to people. Her why was big enough for her to 'man up'.

It was very brave, and I have huge respect for somebody like that. She was absolutely in pieces; she could not even speak. I have never seen someone fall apart so quickly and so dramatically, and yet she then surprised me when she said she had taken a telesales job where she was being rewarded only on her success. So she was not getting paid for making the calls. She was paid on the success rate of achieving the sales.

She wanted to conquer that fear in order to build a portfolio of property for herself and her husband so that they could provide for their family. This enabled them to be able to choose to do what they wished with their time. It was a big enough 'why' for her to be bigger than her fear.

I still tear up when I think about this; I can remember it as clear as day. We sat outside rather than inside so she could have plenty of air. We made those initial calls when she was listening in to me, making those calls in the workshop. She then immersed herself in an environment where she was literally forced to make those calls.

I recall at the time when I was starting out in sales in the early 1980s, I had to lock myself in a room where I was not going to get interrupted by anybody else. I had to really steel myself to make those calls; it was something I had to build up over the years.

There are still people today that I sometimes tremble at the prospect of picking the phone up to. But I know that in every situation where I've done that, it has been better to talk than not to talk.

Name badges

With name badges, use a name you would like to be called. So often I see people with something that only their mother would call them when they are angry.

My name is Tim, but my mother when she was cross with me as a child would say, "Timothy!"

I like to be called Tim; I am actually quite uncomfortable with being called Timothy. I am not going to put Timothy on a name badge just as I am not going to put Timothy on my Linkedin or Facebook profile.

I think the important thing is that these social networks are just an online version of an offline meeting. Whether it is a casual meeting for coffee or a more structured networking meeting, it is still social. Property is about engaging people, understanding what their problems are, and figuring a solution to it.

How to find investors online

There are many opportunities for finding investors online. Probably I've had most success on LinkedIn, and again it's about planting a garden that will attract the right kind of people. So make sure that your profile gives the right sort of message, and make sure that it is kept current and up to date, and by posting relevant articles and posts that engage with people. I think this word 'engagement' is important. Remember, you're showing an interest in what other people are doing, but also sharing in a non-threatening way what you're doing.

LinkedIn I guess for me has been the most successful. Facebook is starting to transition towards a more businesslike environment, particularly with some of the business pages that now proliferate and some of the groups and pages that you can connect in with. Again, it's about engaging with people rather than jumping into bed with them straight away.

I think by understanding who you want to be working with on your projects will help to guide you to the kinds of places that they congregate. So, if you want to work with people who are already property investors, you would spend time and effort and energy in property investor networking groups. If on the other hand, you want to be perhaps in a more business environment, you'd spend time and effort in business groups. So, it's about identifying who you are, and who you want to be dealing with, that will help to guide you towards the right type of environment.

What to put in your online profile

I would expect to see a proper, professional headshot against a plain background, particularly on LinkedIn, not a family shot or taken at the Christmas party. It needs to be something where somebody would recognise you if they met you.

You need to appear as somebody might expect to meet you in perhaps a business setting. So, if in a business setting you normally wear a jacket and tie, that's the image you would portray. If on the other hand like me, you prefer an open neck perhaps with a jacket, that's the image that you should be portraying. So, appear as people would expect to find you in a business environment.

If you're doing that, you're already breaking down the barriers. You're building rapport with somebody even though you haven't necessarily met them. So if they do at some point meet you in the future, they almost feel as if they know who you are because they've seen you on your profile, or perhaps you've done a video or a blog that they're tuning into.

So, getting your profile picture right is really important.

If you're a woman, you should dress as you would expect to be found in a business setting. If you were to meet in a reasonably formal business environment, how would you present yourself? So, if your normal attire is make-up and nicely arranged hair and brooches and all the rest of it, then yes, by all means, that's the sort of image that you should put forward.

Case Study 4

My next client was sending out letters to HMO landlords in his specific target areas and was sending out about 1200 letters a month to his list of HMO landlords. The way he was doing this, he was using his own laser printer; he was printing out 1200 or so letters, and he was then folding those letters, putting them into envelopes, writing the envelope, and sticking a second-class stamp on it.

Now, at the time, a second-class stamp was, I think, 57p, and obviously, you've got the cost of the paper, the ink, the laser, the envelope, but more than that, you've got the time that it was taking to do all of those things. As this client had a day job as a consultant, he had a limited amount of time in the evening after his children were in bed to be able to do property-related activities.

Because I've got experience in the printing industry (I spent nearly 25 years in the printing industry), we started brainstorming ideas about how we could maybe make this more effective. This is the beauty of having more than one brain looking at a given situation, a given challenge. So what we established was that it was possible to just send an electronic file to a direct mailing house and for a total delivery cost of 39p including the postage, including the paper, including the envelope, including all the printing. We saved him way over half of what he was spending each month on his printing and mailing costs, just in one very simple, easy-to-implement idea.

Not only did it save him money, but it doubled the amount of time that he had available. It was taking him two weeks of his available time each month to do all the printing, to do all of the stuffing in the envelopes, to do all of the sticking the stamps on and putting it in the post box, even with help from his babysitter. So it freed up half of his month to be thinking about more creative ways of working within what he was doing; it allowed him to spend more time in researching possible properties. That one idea was life-transforming.

What that allowed him to do then was to go from having just plain mail, which of course everybody's doing, to doing what we call 'lumpy mail'. So we hit upon the idea of putting a peppermint teabag into the mailing and writing a nice story about peppermint tea and how relaxing it was and writing a story that alluded to the fact that it would be more relaxing and less stressful for landlords to be using Peppermint Property to manage their properties than it would by doing it themselves.

So it was a very powerful and memorable message, which instantly achieved him great results from what he was doing. So he immediately got access to one landlady who'd got 13 properties available for management. We also repurposed the letter and put postings on social media which gained him more or less immediately another opportunity and was something seen by over two and a half thousand people.

So again, simple ideas, taking action, and seeing amazing results. That's just by looking at what the challenges are, addressing them and working together to look at, what are the options? What might be a better way of doing this?

Although that's not the core focus of what I do, because we

are looking at goals and how to achieve them, and using my extensive knowledge not just within property but in life in general, we're able to tap into that knowledge and that experience and also my network to be able to facilitate things like this.

How to choose a high-impact photo

Businesslike is best rather than casual. And you need to have a head and shoulders photo, not a full body shot because you need to be able to recognise somebody. That's really crucial. You're in somebody's office or front room, but actually, you're on the computer. So, what they're seeing and what they're relating to is the image that you're putting there. If you can't make out who the person is, or you wouldn't recognise them as a result of looking at their profile picture, it's not doing its job properly. This goes for company logos too. If you are connecting with a person, how will you recognise them if they have an anonymous company logo! Remember these are Social Networks, not business platforms. People buy people, and property is very much a people business.

What to highlight on your online profile

It's important that the name by which you want to be known should be the name that you put on your profile. So for example, my proper name is Timothy, but everybody knows me as Tim. So I would put Tim on my LinkedIn profile rather than Timothy because that's what I'm expecting people to call me. This is about building relationships and nurturing those relationships. If I present myself as Timothy, but actually when you meet me I say, "No, it's Tim," I'm not doing the job properly. I'm potentially confusing and alienating people right at the outset, and you know what they say about first impressions!

Equally, if I've got lots of qualifications, actually I'm not really interested in that as part of my name at the top. So, say for accountants or solicitors where they may well have qualifications and letters after their name, that's not the place for it. In terms of the description of how they portray themselves, it needs to be really succinct, and a good example of this is to take a look at my own LinkedIn profile.

LinkedIn Profile top tips

When you are editing your profile on LinkedIn, follow these simple guidelines.

Intro:

First Name: what people call you. I'm Tim not Timothy so that is what appears on my profile.

Last Name: just your last name, not a string of qualifications and letters. No one cares, and this is not the place for them. Include this in the summary.

Headline: make it catchy, and make sure it is not too long. Make sure it is all visible and highlight with stars or asterisks to make it stand out. This is where you give people the benefits of working with you, not that you are a director of xyz property Ltd.

Summary: more detailed than the headline. Share more about what you do and how you can help people. Include a call to action and a list of specialities – these act as tags for people searching for your skill set.

Keep it fresh – revisit this regularly to keep it updated. It's amazing how quickly it can become stale and out of date.

Top mistakes to avoid with your profile

People sometimes put a company logo in their profile picture. They perhaps use a name that's not the name by which they're known. They've got a profile heading that's not commensurate with what they're actually really doing, and what they're trying to do.

LinkedIn has changed quite a lot, and the whole user experience is different. This can be quite frustrating, particularly if you are not yet a regular user. It is well worth getting some basic training and guidance on setting up a powerful profile. If people search on your name, your LinkedIn profile will come up, so it's essential to get it right. If were to do a Google search on my name, for example, my LinkedIn profile would be quite high up on that.

Work on your elevator pitch.

Telling people everything you've done in the last 20 years isn't a good idea. It's about being selective, things that are relevant. Work out what is likely to be the most relevant to your desired audience. I'm now 56, clearly I've got a lot of life experience, I've tried a lot of things. Some of that experience is relevant and some of it's not, and you've got to decide really what is going to be relevant to the kind of person who's going to be attracted to you and what's irrelevant.

Okay, so if somebody was to ask me who I was and what I was doing, my elevator pitch might go something like this. "I'm Tim Matcham, The Property Finance Coach, I show you how to systematically attract more investor finance for your property deals than you thought possible. Connect with me to establish whether I can help you accelerate your property journey."

Think about the message you want to convey and what call to action you want to include. You need to tell people what to do, as mentioned previously sometimes, people are very slow on the uptake if not given very precise instructions.

How to get remembered after a networking meeting

Following up is crucial. Always, always follow up with an email, a phone call or some sort of note. You might also want to arrange to meet up for a more in-depth conversation or perhaps a virtual coffee on a video conference at an agreed time. You might have a business card with a photo on it so that people remember you. Talk confidently about what you're doing, but without being in anyone's face about it. I think people get turned off if you're too pushy and come across too much as a second-hand car salesman, or a double-glazing salesman type of approach.

People are more interested if you're sharing examples of what you've done or what you aspire to do. Be enthusiastic, not pushy. Show that you have a professional approach.

"When you have a goal in mind, start taking action. What is wrong with NOW!"

"Oh God, I didn't really want to talk to that person ..."

There are times I've come away from a networking meeting and thought, "Oh God, I didn't really want to talk to that person." There are occasions where sometimes you get a very clear sense that it's not a good match and not a good fit for what your values are. So, in that sort of situation, if you're feeling uncomfortable about a meeting, there's a marvellous word, and it's "No." You know, there's nothing forcing you to have to do something – whether that's working with somebody or anything else in life. It's about finding people that you're comfortable with and sometimes, particularly when you start out, there's a tendency to want to grab everything that's available without really giving much thought to the fit, and that can be a mistake. This is one of my personal biggest learnings. I always felt there was a need to please everyone all of the time, and this is just not a realistic expectation and leads to unnecessary stress and often failed collaborations. Do yourself a favour, and be clear about both who you want to say yes to and also for whom "No" is the best response for both parties.

Sometimes, you try to bend over backwards to please somebody, and the more you bend and try to be flexible and move away from your system, you're moving away from your values and you're losing your authenticity which is really important because you're trying to be somebody that you're not. We are human beings, not human *doings,* so consider who you need to be in order to attract the right people. In every occasion, the answer should be: yourself.

Earlier on in this book, I mentioned creating the list of the 30 unique points about yourself, and it's that authenticity that people are buying into. So, if you're deviating from that and trying to pretend to be something that you're not in order to gel with somebody who perhaps doesn't have those same values, you're not creating a valid connection. It's one that will always cause you problems, and it's better to address that at an earlier stage of a relationship and really be thoughtful and mindful as to what the relationship will look like. That's the purpose of doing all the exercises right at the start so that you get a real fit for who you are and who the people are that you want to do deal with.

So, when you do encounter people that don't fit those criteria, you don't waste lots of time and effort and energy pursuing something that's never really going to work, never really going to be successful. It can be quite hard, particularly at the beginning when you are perhaps seeing the opportunity to secure a deal, and you can't because you haven't got the money. But there's somebody who has got the money, and just by being a bit flexible, you might be able to secure a deal with them. This is a question obviously for your own personal values, but for me, if I don't feel right and the relationship doesn't feel right, my tendency these days is to be strong enough to be able to walk away from it rather than feel that I have to pursue that particular line. Frequently these 'opportunities' don't work out quite the way you were hoping.

My own Hobson's Choice

I've certainly got examples of when I should've said no. There was one situation that I remember very clearly a few years ago when I was faced with a very harsh choice, and I likened it to having a gun held to my head at the edge of a cliff. If I jumped, I wasn't going to be shot, and if I didn't jump, I'd be shot. I think it's known as Hobson's Choice – I didn't feel as if I had the option to say "No." In hindsight, it would've been a much, much better decision and saved me years of heartache. Taking time to step back and seek a second opinion and properly evaluating the situation.

But then that wouldn't have allowed me the learning opportunities that I've had to be able to share my knowledge and wisdom with people today. So, yes, it was a hard thing to deal with, and that was literally to do with trying to please too many people – trying to please everybody – thinking I was helping, when in fact, in reality, I was probably adding fuel to the fire. That was quite tough to deal with. I'm a strong believer in taking responsibility for your own actions; I'm not about pointing the finger of blame. This was me being naïve, and I was flattered to be asked to do what I was doing and without really evaluating the consequences before going ahead and understanding what the implications were of what was being asked of me.

It's OK to make mistakes along the way

My journey over the last few years has given me the experience to be able to write this now; my lessons have come from many, many years, and in life, I guess we all go through experiences. I was lucky enough to go to one of the top private schools in the country, and we were brought up to believe that we couldn't fail at anything. I remember the head teacher describing us as "the cream of the country" in that we were rich and thick. I remember him standing in the pulpit of the chapel and preaching to us. It's possibly the only sermon I think I've remembered in my life, and that's now over 40 years ago. I can still remember it as clear as day; I remember where I was sitting, and I can remember the posture of the person speaking.

The whole point is that we were brought up in a very privileged environment; World War III could have been going on down the road, and we really wouldn't have known about it. So it was very protected; a very closed environment. The belief was both at home and at school, we simply couldn't fail. Failure wasn't a word that was ever mentioned or discussed. It was something that was pretty much a taboo subject. Fast forward to 1999, I was running a small print company, and we did very well, but not well enough. We had massive overheads, and we simply couldn't meet the cost of the overheads.

Like so many start-up businesses, we didn't make it through the first two years. This was a massive, massive shock to my system because, as I said, we were brought up to believe that we couldn't fail at anything, and here I was busy crashing a company at quite significant costs. That left me in a very bad place. I went into massive depression, shortly after the birth of our fourth child, and I'm told I spent six months literally curled up in a ball, crying. This is not a good place to be, a very dark place. I think it's Richard Branson who talks about, "failing your way to success." That wasn't a view that was commonly held back at the turn of the millennium, or at least not in the circles I had in life. So, coming to terms with that loss – it wasn't the company that had failed, it was *me* that had failed. It was very personal; I associated that failure with something wrong with me, rather than the system or the business.

It was very, very personal because nobody explained to me that there was any difference. I was pumped with lots of very toxic drugs in an effort to try and get me out of this depression, and in fact, I've spent many years since trying to detox those chemicals and toxins that I put into my body now that I'm much more enlightened. But, at that time, I didn't know any better. So, taking the lessons from that and over the following 13-14 years, I grew to understand that there were alternatives.

Taking responsibility for things that are associated with you is a far better, more enlightened way of moving forward; especially accepting responsibility for things that haven't gone much according to plan. We are human, we do make mistakes, and that's OK. And it's not just OK; it's actually to be almost encouraged.

One of my coaches said to me: "You'll learn nothing from my successes, but you'll learn everything from my failures and where things haven't gone right." Because those learnings are far more powerful than if everything goes through perfectly. I think that's a really powerful lesson in accepting responsibility and understanding that we are in control of our own destiny, and perhaps more so today than we've ever been.

I rarely, if ever, watch television, read the newspaper or listen to the radio. Instead, I choose to listen to motivational podcasts, or audio books if I'm driving. So I don't expose myself to situations over which I don't really have any particular control, but I do focus on the actions that I can control and that can affect what I do on a day-to-day basis. Every minute of every day, I have a choice as to what I can do and how I can behave and what outcomes I can expect from that. I can choose whether I'm happy or sad; and who would choose to be sad?

It really is a choice, and I think once you understand that and that a failure is just that – it's not *you* that's failed, it's an object or an action that's the failure, not you. It's not personal. Providing you don't keep doing the same thing and expecting a better result, then you're going to learn and move forward. I think that's one of the benefits of having coaches and people you can reflect off of; having peers that think in a similar way to you. You've got that ability to reflect off them and just challenge the situation perhaps that you've found yourself in, whatever that might be, and understand where the value is in it. That's kind of cool really. My beliefs and my *"why"* for doing this are to be able to offer that help and support to people so they don't have to go through the darkness that I experienced; to help them to be able to shine brightly. Nothing gives me more pleasure than to see people that I'm working with excel at what they're doing, and I know that I helped them and guided them to that success. That's awesome for me. The feeling of watching someone else reach their goals is a very powerful motivator for me, so rewarding to see that success blossom.

The importance of goal setting

One of the first things that you need to do will be to look at setting your goals. For me, this goes back to my own story of running the New York Marathon and having a blue line to follow. Running a marathon is a pretty big goal, and in a way, it's a like a property journey. You know when you're running the marathon where the start line is and where the finish line is. They paint a blue line so that you can follow that all the way through the marathon and so you don't get diverted. The point of it is that you know where the start is; you know where you are now, and you know where you are trying to get to. It is filling that gap and taking the next step.

So when you are setting out on your journey, quite a lot of people come to me and say, "Right, I'd like to raise some money. I need money for my next property deal." My question is, "What are you trying to achieve? How much money do you want to borrow?" and "What would that mean to you if you can get that money? How does it contribute to where you are going, to your end goal?" Ideally, you will have an understanding of where we are now, and you want to get to. You should not be like the guy, who when asked for directions to get to somewhere, said: "I would not start from here!"

This is about being very clear where you are, and what the next steps are in your journey, and what is the end point you want to get to. This is going to be very different from everyone else because success means different things to different people.

You may not know all the steps in your journey, but if you have got a vision of what the end place looks like, it is easier to get the support of people along the way to help you stay on that track, and to stay on the 'blue line'. Occasionally, you may wander off it, but because you know where your track is, it is much easier to get back on course and to refocus and re-energise. Understanding *who* you are is important, but also *where* you are now and where you are going to is critical.

Setting your goals

There are many different ways to set up goals. As a rule, though, the more specific you can make your goals, the better. Writing it down will help you bring it to life and revisit it later.

Start out by defining what you want to achieve. Identify why this is important to you. What resources will you need and who else will you need to make it a reality. Few of us can achieve goals on our own, be as specific as possible. The greater the detail, the better.

Just saying you want to be financially free doesn't cut the mustard. Put numbers against it, how many properties, of what type? Yielding what sort of returns? You are giving yourself something then to know when you have achieved this goal. You will also be helping your support team better understand what you are striving for, whether that is family or business associates and your power team.

How likely are you to achieve it? Is it something that someone else has already achieved? Might you require outside assistance to achieve this goal? What would that look like?

Does achieving this goal make sense to you or is it something a bit random? The greater sense it makes, the more likely you are to stay on track and keep taking the next step to achieve it.

It is also important to define when you are going to achieve this goal by; otherwise, you are just dreaming! You may need to break a big goal into smaller milestones so that you can see you are taking the right course.

Building your story ...

I met with a friend at a recent property networking event who was achieving a good deal of success raising finance; I dug a bit deeper, and what he was doing is using Facebook really effectively to build a story so that his friends and his contacts know exactly what he is doing.

He has built a story over time and is sharing his experience, his knowledge, his journey with his contacts on social media. So when it comes to the time when he needs finance, he is able to tap into money easily because he has built a story, and he has built the trust. He is working with people who know him, and he is telling everybody what he is doing so people are buying into his story. This perfectly illustrates that by following the steps outlined in this book, you can achieve success in raising private finance.

He told me, "Look, I've raised a lot of money, and it is from people I know." I said, "Great. Fantastic." It just reinforces the message that: 'people buy people'. They are not buying the project; they are buying into this particular person's story.

So help others to understand what *you* are doing and share *your* story, be it your ups and downs, and the things that go right as well as the things that go wrong, and so on. This makes you more real and authentic, and people can relate to that.

It was interesting to hear about somebody else's experiences as he was really endorsing himself. I do not think he realised what he was doing necessarily, but I could instantly recognise in him that he was doing all the right things, and he maybe just needed a little bit of guidance on how to roll that out and scale it up.

People buy people ...

I'm often asked the question: "Why would someone invest in me?"

I think most people may feel an element of doubt as to why someone would be interested in investing in them. You really need to dig deep with this because if you do not know why somebody would invest in you, nobody else is going to know either! It is really important to understand why a deal with you works and what would make it attractive. Put yourself in the investor's shoes to understand the kind of things they would be looking for.

So if you do not know why, it would be difficult for somebody else to buy into it if you have not got a clue. It is about valuing your time and yourself, which is why I recommend that you go through exercise to understand what makes you unique.

If you have a situation where you are in doubt about the deal you are offering because you are not sure it is not good enough, you are probably asking people *not* to invest in you.

This is for your own protection as well as the investors because if you are entering into the deal and don't know why it works, the question is: why are you doing it and inviting investors to be part of it?

It is all part of the due diligence process, and maybe you need to speak to a specialist or advisor to help you analyse your deal and to validate it and make sure it is the good deal that you think it is. Understand why it is good and what the risk factors are. What are the areas of risk with the deal? What can go wrong, and how would you deal with those aspects? Showing that you understand there is risk and understand how to manage it will always stand you in good stead.

So many times people look at the good aspects of what can happen or might happen, but they fail to take into account the areas that perhaps can go wrong and make allowance for those by way of a plan or contingency.

> ### Due diligence
>
> - Speak to a specialist or advisor.
> - Analyse your deal to check it's as good as you think it is.
> - Understand why it is a good deal.
> - Understand the risk factors.
> - What are the things that can go wrong?
> - How would you deal with those things?

Financial Conduct Authority (FCA) Legislation PS13/3

If you want to do this systematically and reliably, you need to build something more profound and create relationships. The rules and regulations have changed a bit now, for the FCA the legislation that is known as PS13/3 is you're not allowed to do certain things when promoting property deals.

You need to be very careful about not flaunting rules and regulations when you are attracting money for investment purposes. This lengthy document is neither easy to read or understand and interpret, though, which doesn't help! If in doubt, seek the advice of a finance specialist, and make sure you don't get caught out.

Won't it seem like I'm begging for money?

I think this is a really common misconception and a massive limiting belief probably for most people. In fact, it is one of the biggest limiting beliefs to overcome. This is the idea you are handing a begging bowl out and in some ways desperate for the money. You perceive that you are coming across as needy, which in turn repels most investors, so it becomes a self-fulfilling belief.

The way to look at this is to understand the challenges that your possible investor might be facing. So you need to put yourself in their shoes and understand what kind of pain they may be experiencing. Probably the simplest example of this is to look at the current bank rates and building society rates or savings accounts rates at the moment. So, anybody who has got money in the bank, by the time you taken inflation into account, you are actually losing money because the interest rates are so low that they are not getting any sort of meaningful return on the money they have got in the bank or building society.

The major pain is they are just not getting the return or any value out of any funds they have available. So how can you use that?

It comes back to presenting an opportunity, rather than coming across as desperate. If the problem is that they are getting low interest rates, the question to the investor is: "You are getting 1% or less than 1% in the bank, so what interest rate would attract you? What would be something that might inspire you to be interested in investing in a property project?"

This is again asking them the questions, so rather than telling them you are offering X per cent or Y per cent, you are asking them what level would they be interested in. If you have a clear idea in your head as to what level you would be comfortable working with, and if you have got a match, then this is a great opportunity. You may be surprised at how low an interest rate people will be interested in working with you for. It depends on how quickly you want the money and what risks are attached to that.

You also need to understand that just because you are in the property world, and you understand some great rates are achievable, your average property investor might not. Your average investor who does not go along to property meetings is unlikely to understand what returns might be available in property projects. If they are reading newspapers or watching the news on television or listening to it on radio, the kind of information that they will be hearing or receiving is that property generally yields in the region of 5% or 6% returns on capital.

So if you are bowling into a situation and saying to somebody, "Right, I'll offer you 20% or 18%," and their expectation is set by the world they live in and tune into, and they are expecting 8%, by going into 18%, you are terrifying them.

It starts opening up questions and feelings such as, "It is too good to be true? It must be risky." So actually, you are pushing people away rather than attracting them. The way around that is to ask them, "What rate would you be interested in investing in a project? If there was a project like this, what sort of rate would you be interested in working with me on it?"

It goes back to just asking the right questions and being armed with appropriate questions that will allow a potential investor to tell you what they are happy working with. Spend some time now thinking about what questions you might ask a potential investor that would help build a great relationship.

There is nothing to say you have to work with somebody just because they come back to you, and your ideal interest rate is, for argument sake, say 8%, and somebody comes back to you and wants 10%. You have now got a decision to make as to whether your particular project will stand having 10% as an interest rate on the money that you are borrowing. You may then want to do an analysis to work out: if I get the money, and if that is 10% instead of 8%, am I actually still able to do the deal? It just becomes an extra cost, a business cost of doing that deal. You have a decision to make if the extra interest you are being asked to pay is appropriate to allow you to physically do that deal.

Case Study 5

I had a couple come in who recognised that they were being held back by not being able to access private finance. We dug deep into this and had a look at why they held these beliefs, and a lot of it was to do with not being comfortable asking people for money because they saw it as begging, and the idea of asking people for money was seen as coming from a position of desperation and need. They were so wound up with this perception of what it was that they really couldn't break through that belief, because they'd held it, perhaps they'd been brought up to think and believe that borrowing money was a bad thing and not something to be done.

There are sayings such as, 'Neither a borrower nor a lender be'. It is quite ingrained in our history and our way that we're brought up. People see the idea of working with other people's money as breaking that value almost. I think this is where people seem to have their biggest blocks.

So I had a look at this and said, "Okay, why do you hold those beliefs?" We dug deep into it, and then I said, "Okay, so let's change the way that we're looking at this, and rather than looking at it from your perspective as a potential borrower, let's look at it from the perspective of a potential investor. And have a look at what challenges they face as somebody who's got money perhaps in a bank or building society, and what challenges they face given that situation, given that scenario."

We fairly quickly identified that, particularly at the moment, interest rates are very low and that, in fact, if they've got money in a bank or building society, that actually they're losing money because inflation is eating away any benefit that they might be getting as far as interest is concerned. Once we started reframing that, and that it was potentially causing an investor pain, it then became much easier to position their proposition. Rather than begging for money, they were actually doing these people a huge favour because it's massively beneficial to them to have the opportunity, presented in the right way, to be able to look at alternatives that they perhaps weren't aware of previously as a potential opportunity.

Rather than being viewed as something which might make them angry or reticent, they were more likely to be hugely grateful because, for the right opportunity, presented in the right way, this presents them a massive opportunity to move forward rather than backwards.

I think once we had reframed it and positioned it from the investor's viewpoint, this was something that worked really well for both sides. It was something that was mutually beneficial. In fact, you're actually being harder to them and more unkind, if you like, by not offering them the opportunity and not sharing the possibilities with them than you are by presenting it in such a way that it's seen as being beneficial.

So actually, you're doing people a disservice by not sharing the opportunity. I think once you start turning it around like that, and you start looking at the benefits and the upside of it, it becomes easier to perhaps reframe and to get a clearer understanding.

How to break off a conversation without causing offence

Sometimes it's clear that the person you're speaking to at a networking event isn't a good fit, and you're unlikely to work with them in the future. So you will need to break off your conversation in a way that is elegant and polite in order to avoid causing offence.

There is an art to this. If you go to any networking meeting, you are going to find people who want to hog you and monopolize you. This is perhaps because they're terrified of being at the meeting, and they're relieved to have found someone who is going to talk to them and not bite their head off, which is perhaps the preconception that they've come to the meeting with. In this instance, it's very easy just to say, "Look, it's been great talking to you. There's a number of other people here that I'd like to just touch base with. If you've got any questions, do grab me before you go – enjoy the meeting, and I'll see you later." This gives them the opportunity to re-engage with you if they want to.

The other way of doing it is to ask them, "Is there anybody in the room that you'd particularly like to meet or be introduced to?" If you yourself don't happen to know somebody, the easiest thing to do then is to pass them back to the host or one of the helpers of the meeting and just say, "Please can you help X? She's here for the first time and doesn't really know anybody. Can you help introduce her to somebody she's particularly interested in?" That way you help them to meet more people specifically in areas that are of interest to them, and you've given yourself permission to move on, and you've done so in a very elegant way.

You've done this in a way that's kind and not going to upset anybody. The thing to bear in mind is that you're there at a networking meeting with the intention of meeting as many people as possible. You're not there to meet one person and spend the entire evening with them. If you want to spend more time, and you think it might be valuable, you can indicate that – but even people that I do want to talk to, I'll be parting from them in much the same way because I haven't gone to the meeting just to meet one person. I've gone for the purpose of meeting at least five new people; sometimes I go to a meeting, and I might try to meet 10. For some people that would be just too daunting, but for me, heaven is a room of people that I don't know who are all interested in the same thing. I understand that's not everybody's cup of tea. But it is something that you can learn and that you can get good at just by thinking what the basics are; thinking of how you would like to be treated and reflecting that back.

In person or online?

I tend to prefer getting an expression of interest at a meeting, building that relationship and taking it to a coffee or lunch meeting. Or perhaps a site visit works well if you have got existing projects you can show to investors. It's just as easy though to meet virtually on one of the video conferencing apps, and this may well be easier if you have met someone online in the first place. The good thing is that there is no right or wrong here; it's all about what works best for both parties.

"FEAR: False Evidence Appearing Real. Unknown Sometimes expressed as Future Evidence Appearing Real i.e. imagining the worst – how often does this ever manifest? We spend so much time worrying about things that will never happen and if they do won't be as bad as we thought they might be. Live in the present and deal with where you are now, then, take the next step."

I've tried asking for money before, but it did not work. How can I move forward?

First of all, to help you in this situation, I would want to know what approach you have used, and why you feel it did not work. The fact is that there is plenty of money out there, so you are likely to have missed one or more of the steps that I advocate going through in order to secure it. You have perhaps made one of the mistakes I mention, such as arriving at the meeting, bombarding everyone with business cards and then saying, "I've got deals if you've got money. Come and invest in me." But perhaps you have not invested time in that relationship, so it's not really surprising that you have not achieved it. Generally speaking, if you are not succeeding, you are likely to be missing the steps in the process that you need to go through in order to approach people. Or perhaps you are approaching them in a way that it turns them away rather than attracting them.

You need to look at what you are actually doing and what the impact of what you are doing is having on potential investors. It can be about a subtle change in your language, in your tone, in the way something is presented rather than a massive change. It is all very subtle.

It is about reading people; it is about understanding where people have got pain and addressing that pain. So it is about them, not about you. If it is about "me, me, me," all the time, an investor is not going to buy into that. It is about what is in it for them. Why is it attractive to them to be involved in it?

The value of authenticity

You have to come across as confident, but some investors don't like people who are overconfident. It goes back to the list of what makes you unique. Be yourself.

Investors want transparency. They want to know who they are dealing with. This is a people thing, of understanding who you are and what all your qualities are, and this will help you to be authentic. That authenticity is important. If you are trying to be somebody else, if you are uncomfortable with what you are doing, investors will pick up on that.

Avoid jargon ...

When somebody talks to you in technical language, it can become confusing to people who aren't dialled in to that way of thinking and working. I had a conversation with an insurance broker, and I think he talked for nearly half an hour, and I'm not sure I actually understood any of that conversation at all. He was using terminology and assumed I had prior knowledge, and I think he was quite shocked when I said at the end of it, "I haven't understood a word as I don't operate in the world of insurance and the implications of what you're telling me. You might as well be talking in a completely foreign language." Sometimes we need to take a step back and look at simplifying the words we use and the terminology we use and expect others to use.

I had a similar experience when I first started investing in property. I frequently went along to business networking breakfasts, and I went back to one after I had been to a number of property investor meetings. I started using the language I had been using at the property investor meetings in the business breakfast meeting, and it was like I was talking a completely different language, and people were looking at me as if to say, "Tim, we have absolutely no idea what you're talking about." This is because they weren't on the same journey as me. They hadn't explored other possibilities; they were still in their own business world and so, to start introducing terminology like "HMOs" or "buy-to-lets" or "rent to rent" was beyond their level of comprehension because I was using words that meant nothing to them, so they were nervous and wary of it. I remember one lady telling me she was frightened by the words that I was using, which was interesting because she was a very competent businesswoman. She was happy in her own business environment, but when we started talking about something she had no knowledge of and using language she didn't understand, it switched her off very quickly and in fact, frightened her.

Case Study 6

A young lady called Rachel had lined up some potential investor finance but then found that she didn't really have the confidence to take it all the way through because she wasn't sure of the process that she was going through to do it.

So although there was interest from the private investor to invest with her, because neither party really knew what they were doing or how they were doing it, there wasn't the appropriate framework in place to allow them to actually do the transaction.

So it then sort of fell apart. Because they didn't have a reference framework to be able to work to, to actually make sure it happened, the investor then got cold feet and decided that he wasn't prepared to take what he saw as risk because it wasn't presented in a way that showed him how his money was going to be protected and what precautions were being taken.

So it was to do with the presentation of, and understanding, that these questions are things that investors are going to ask and that you need to be prepared for them. And because there wasn't the preparation there, the opportunity slipped by, and they lost that opportunity and hadn't had the confidence to go back, although they now had more

---

experience. I think they were just starting out with their property journey and perhaps didn't feel that they really knew enough about it.

Part of what I help clients to look at is how, if you don't have experience yourself, you can leverage the power of a team that does have that experience and can help you to achieve these things. It's about understanding what things you can have in place in order to make these things work.

Avoid alienating people

Keep it as simple as possible. Understand where the people that you are communicating with sit in the education curve and the knowledge curve and think back to perhaps a time when you weren't involved in property investment. I remember before I got involved in the property world, I thought there was literally only one way to invest in property which was to go along to an estate agent with a cheque book and ask them to sell me a house which I could then rent out: "Oh, and by the way, once you've sold it to me, can you rent it out for me?" I thought that was the only way to do it because I had no knowledge of all the other possibilities that were out there because I hadn't educated and immersed myself in the world of property.

At the time, the fact that I was even interested in property investment made me different to other people because property is seen by some as a dark art because they don't understand it, and they haven't taken time to understand it. You need to be aware of that when you're talking about projects and about opportunities; just be aware that some people aren't going to be as excited about it or as motivated about it as you are. That's OK. That's where you are digging the garden to sow the seeds of interest in people perhaps who haven't been interested before, but who are now intrigued because of your story and how you're telling it. You're aiming to tell it in a way that is simple and easy to understand for people who are not in the property world. If you use frightening language and inflated interest rates, they're less likely to be interested.

How to move things along to the next level

After the initial pleasantries, you will need to transition things to the next level. You will need to test the water so to speak to see if they are interested in investing or if they have money to invest.

Is everybody you approach going to have money? The answer is no.

Is everybody who has money going to want to invest with you? The answer is no.

So it is about finding a match and understanding how much you need. What you need the money for will help you narrow it down.

> **The kind of questions that you want to be asking at this stage are:**
>
> - "What challenges do you face on your property journey at the moment?"
> - "So you want to invest in property, what is stopping you?"

- "What are the blockers that are holding you up at the moment?"

- "Is it finding deals? Is it finding money?"

- "What are the things that are preventing you from taking action?"

From this, you are getting a picture of what things are holding them back. These must not be the first questions you ask; this is a kind of progression. You ask what kind of strategy they are involved with; what are their goals? If they are looking to achieve a certain something, what is holding them back?

What are the blockers? What are the biggest challenges they face at the moment? And if you perhaps start to get promising answers, a great question to follow with is, "... and what else?"

So they might say, "Well, finding great deals is a problem." You go, "So what deals are you looking for?" They say, "I am looking for three-bed terraces that I can convert into six bed HMO, in a specific area." So here, you ask, "And what else is causing you not being able to move forward?"

Keep asking that question, "And what else ... And what else?" It is a great way of drawing out people and getting them to think about what challenges they face at the moment.

All this time, you are engaging with them, you are building trust and building rapport. It might be one of the things that they talk about you can help them with or maybe you know somebody else you have been talking to in a similar meeting that might be able to help them.

It is not just property meetings; it is important to recognise the same technique is used in business meetings. You may need to tone it down because clearly, people in a business meeting may not be interested in, or less knowledgeable in, investing in property. But it is still about asking questions and asking them what challenges they face. You can steer the conversation quite well with practice. I am not suggesting you are going to be able to do this first time around, but say if somebody is in employment, what challenges does that present? How long are they going to work for? What is their pension provision like? What are the other things they have looked at investing in?

There are ways of drawing out people, not as the first conversation, but over time. It is about building that rapport and building that relationship over time.

At what stage do you set things down in writing?

If there is an expression of interest, you can move on to setting down a proposal in writing. Even if you are not getting an expression of interest from the person you are talking to, you should remain mindful the whole time of them at work and the people they might associate with. I recommend that you think about the wider picture the whole time because it is not just about the people you know, it is the people that they know and their network as well.

In terms of actually putting something in writing, this is probably best when they have made an expression of interest so that they have something to look at. If you have not got an existing deal or something you have actually done, there is nothing to stop you from putting an example deal together so that people can get a flavour for the kind of deal you might be looking at.

It does not need to be something you've actually done, but it can be due diligence on an example of a typical property.

This goes back to identifying what kind of deal you would like. If you are confident of what your ideal deal looks like and what parameters you want to be working in, you will find that really easy then to convey it on a single sheet of A4, with perhaps a picture to show what the property will look like, but it is something people can relate to. This can just be an outline sketch of what the property is and what the proposition is. Be prepared then, if there is a further expression of interest, to go into more depth. But avoid bombarding people with massive amounts of data to begin with.

You are sharing an idea to see whether it is something they might be interested in.

What to include and what to leave out.

In any deal, there is a massive amount of information. So you have to decide what to keep in and what to take out; which highlights you choose to put before investors. You need to select information that is going to be the most relevant, exciting, and engaging that is going to make them invest in you.

Property deals are many and varied, so there is not a single blueprint that you can use. But a clear indication of the cost of purchase if you are purchasing a property: the cost of any works that you need to do; if you are looking at renting it, how much will it cost to do that? What is the timescale involved? What are the risks? What are the things you have no control over? What are you going to do in order to minimize and mitigate the risks. If you do not acknowledge there are risks, investors are going to worry that you have not identified what the risks are, which is very scary, or that you are pretending there are not going to be any risks attached to this deal, which diminishes credibility and trust.

What investors will want to know:

- the cost of any works needed;

- annual rent and costs (if renting out)

- timescale

- risk factors

- risk mitigation

- how much investment is required

Most investors or anyone who knows anything about property would acknowledge things can and do go wrong, and it is just affirming that because, generally speaking, one of the biggest things that come out time and time again with investors is *transparency*. People want to know you know what you are doing! Sharing that you understand and can manage risk is a massive bonus when working with investors.

So the other thing that is important is looking at the exit strategies. Please note that this is in the plural – strategies – because if you only have one exit and then something happens that makes that particular exit unviable for whatever reason, you need to have alternatives. You have to be comfortable in the worst case scenario that the worst possible thing that could happen is still "fine", and it would allow you to repay the loan from the investor. You need to identify what is the worst thing that can happen and be comfortable that they may have three or four different exits. You may not choose to go that route in ideal circumstances, but if you have to, what are the implications? Because an investor would want to know what is the worst-case scenario. What risks are they exposing themselves to? They want to know that you understand there are risks and what you will do and what can you do to address these.

Don't hide things under the carpet

In other words, do not be afraid to face worst-case scenarios. This is a strength rather than a weakness. You might think it is better to hide negatives under the carpet and avoid discussing them, but this will only have the opposite effect.

Facing worst-case scenarios and discussing them is actually a great strength. It is essential to investor relations, building that level of trust. If you acknowledge that there are challenges, and you are on top of them, rather than waiting for the problem to happen, this is more likely to reassure investors. For example, is it easier to address a problem before or after it happens? Afterwards, you are picking up the pieces. It is far better to acknowledge there may be potential problems and to identify a number of possible solutions to deal with this and show that you are working on the case.

What if you dislike a person?

Occasionally, you'll find someone who is a good fit as an investor, and who has the money and inclination to invest, but you get a gut feeling that you do not actually like them as a person. This leaves you with a difficult decision as to whether to accept the money they are offering.

I personally would not accept. But if you were in a state of desperation, you might accept money from somebody you do not have a good relationship with. I personally prefer to work with people I like rather than people I do not like. But, of course, that does not always happen. I know from experience that it is always easier to deal with people you have rapport with and can talk openly with.

Most of the challenges that I have faced have come from being with people who, for whatever reason, I have not gelled with.

Property is a people business, and relationships are important. Again, it depends on your reason "why".

I know some people who are happy to put up with less than a good relationship because they are very driven, but to me, it seems like setting yourself up for trouble.

Red flags early on in the negotiating process

Look out to see if the investor is making reasonable requests or unreasonable requests in terms of the hoops they want you to jump through in order for you to secure the deal. These may be a personal preference of an investor, and you cannot really get around that.

If you have identified in your checklist who your ideal investment partner would be, in theory, this should make it easier to find the person you are comfortable and happy to be dealing with. If you do find somebody who does not match with that checklist, then perhaps think again.

The messages you send out, and the way you conduct yourself, should be attracting the people that match that profile. That is why that checklist is important, so you really need to drill that down.

How to decide your rates of interest

You need to know what numbers work for you, and what can be flexible, so beyond what number will this not be a viable project for you? What is the impact of the project over-running by six months; if you have budgeted for borrowing over a £100,000 for 12 months and you are not ready to exit for another six months, what is the impact? So you need to be comfortable with the impact of the interest rate over time and understand what parameters you are comfortable with working within.

There are a number of options here. One is to say, "We have got an opportunity, but actually it is not that high risk," in which case you offer a lower interest rate. Or you say: "We have an opportunity which has a higher element of risk," and offer a higher rate of interest is because there are higher risks attached. So you are indicating to the person involved that this is either a lower risk project with a lower rate of interest or vice versa.

How long can you borrow the money for?

Again, this varies enormously. It is about understanding what the investor is prepared to put up with, which means: what they are looking for or what they are paying?

Some are willing to tie their money up for, say, five years. But, more generally, people are happier for a shorter term. They typically want 6-12 months. Is it possible to extend this time? Yes, absolutely when trust has been built.

This is about building that relationship, building that rapport, keeping them informed of what is happening. It is better to know if the investor wants their money back when you are not ready sooner rather than later as you may need to approach someone else to replace that investor before you exit that project.

The importance of keeping investors informed

I would recommend keeping in regular contact with your investors so that they know what is happening. It's easy to overlook this when you are busy. But you need to contact them at least once a month, minimum. Or, you may want to do a weekly report. It depends on the project, what stage it's at, and how it is going. It's important all the way through to be open and honest.

The best-case scenario

In a best-case scenario, you should be able to borrow money for as long as you actually need to. It is just the matter of matching yourself with the right person who is aligned with what you need for your project.

Generally speaking, you will find it easier to acquire money for a shorter term rather than a longer term. But there are people out there who quite frequently will buy into a five-year bond. You can also offer them a bonus for keeping their money in your project for say, five years. You have to consider it from their point of view: "What would make it attractive to keep my money there for five years?"

There are many tools you can use. Interest rates are one. Do they want monthly interest or annual? What bonus might there be? What is likely to make it an attractive proposition?

If you are doing a development project that is not generating cash flow, are you prepared to give a higher rate of interest in order to pay at the end of the project, rather than as you go through it? Because as you are not generating income, you are effectively paying their interest out of the money you borrow. You need to make that clear because you can go to an investor and say, "This is a development project, we are not generating cash flow because we have not ten or twenty rooms to let, so I will be paying your interest out of the money you've lent me."

Most investors will not see sense in that. They will understand that and what you are doing and how you are doing it, but they would possibly want a bonus perhaps at the end of it.

It is about negotiating the parameters that you are happy and comfortable with for the particular project you are looking at.

This is why I recommend loans rather than doing joint ventures. A loan is a much simpler arrangement between two people. It is a fixed amount of money for a fixed length of time for a fixed rate of interest.

The whole thing is very clear; it is just black or white without discussion or arguments about what other expectations are. This is why the FCA, is so much more lenient about these than joint ventures.

How much money can you borrow?

There is nothing to stop you from borrowing whatever you want, but it is more about finding the person who has the money and is in the position to lend it. Again, it comes to identifying who your ideal investor is. If you are looking for millions, then talking to your Aunt Jude who has got £50,000 stashed under her mattress because she does not believe in the bank is not going to work. You are barking up the wrong tree in terms of the type of person you are trying to approach.

Who sorts out the paperwork?

I have experienced both ways. Frequently, I will present the loan agreement and present it as my standard loan agreement.

I say to the investors, "This is the standard document I have used on a number of occasions with other investors."

However, it is important to offer them the option of creating their own loan agreement. Providing that their requests are reasonable, I will agree with it.

So if they want to use their loan agreement, and they are not requesting something unreasonable of me, if they prefer to use their own documentation, then I am fine with that.

The first time I borrowed somebody else's paperwork, I had it checked it out by my lawyer to make sure it did not put the lender or me under any unnecessary obligations.

So we got started with somebody else's paperwork that got amended by my lender's solicitors too. We added things into it that gave extra reassurance to the lenders. All of these documents were subject to improvement. You have to come up with something that works comfortably for both parties.

You do not need to get bogged down in paperwork; there are lots of templates readily available on the Internet or from other people in property or at networking meetings. You will find that there is usually someone available and willing to help you.

But I would always advocate that you get it checked by an independent legal professional. It is important that you recognise these are legal documents, and you need to understand the implications of what is written. And for this purpose, you need to get independent legal advice.

How much does it cost?

It depends on the solicitor you choose, but it can be anywhere between £500 and £1,000. This is all part of the cost of borrowing, and the cost of business.

I have my standard legal document, but I always offer the other party the opportunity to put it past their solicitors, and I also sometimes I pick up the bill on that. This will depend a bit on how much is being lent and for how long. Clearly picking up massive bills on a small short term loan may be prohibitive. Ultimately, you have a choice.

There are some instances, particularly when we are borrowing from pension funds, where the other party will present paperwork for signature.

So once you have come up with a standard document and paid a solicitor to check it, you can use the same documentation again and again. Obviously, you will need to personalise it for different investors.

What if you cannot pay the money back; what is the worst thing that could happen?

People need to understand that there are risks attached to borrowing money and investing in property. Having a disclaimer on documents is a good idea so that people and investors are aware of the risks.

Money Laundering

Money laundering is one of the things that has come to the fore more recently and become more of an issue. If you are taking money for investment, or if you are personally investing in property, your solicitor should be asking you (and your investors) about, "Where did you get the money from?" So it is important you know where the money has come from in the first place. Is it from an inheritance, a redundancy payment, savings, a divorce settlement, for example.

Certainly, if you buy a property, the solicitor will want to know where the money is coming from and to have seen it in a specific account for a certain length of time. If you're working with investor's finance, you need to be very clear with your solicitors – it's a conversation to have before you start all of this. You need to be very clear and transparent with the solicitors, and they may well guide you on the money laundering aspect of it.

Look at getting professional advice. Work closely with your solicitor to share with them what you're doing and how you're doing it, and use them for guidance, particularly on the first couple of projects. Just be aware that there are hoops to jump through; it's not necessarily a straightforward process.

Hoops to jump through

With any project, there are going to be a certain number of hoops to jump through – money laundering checks, paperwork, etc. – so you are understandably going to be worried about losing your investor if there are too many hoops.

To alleviate this, I think it's about sharing with them *why* you're doing all of these things; that you are acting in an ethical and a responsible manner. That you're making sure both sides are protected. There's lots of supporting material that should encourage rather than discourage the investor. I think if you're trying to secure a deal too quickly or cut corners, that will raise alarm bells. You're demonstrating a professional approach; you're using professional people – rather than adding to their fear. You're allaying their fear because you're going through a due diligence process that shows professionalism and shows that you care about working with them. Rather than just chucking their money into a bank account, point out that you want to do this properly so you're protecting them, and this is the procedure you normally go through. Tell them: "We work with our team to make sure this process goes smoothly." Offer assurance the whole time by indicating this is a normal process and is there for their protection.

How to present your property investment plans

There are a great many ways to present your property investment plans. It's not just about putting a PowerPoint slide presentation together or writing it all down on a bit of paper. You can produce a little video if you want to.

I think this comes back to authenticity; it's what you feel

comfortable with. We're obviously living in an age where video is very powerful, providing it's relevant and has a value to people. The one thing about video is you can't speed-read it; therefore, different forms of communication will appeal to different people. Again, this stresses the importance of identifying the kinds of people you want to be connecting with. Are they people who are going to respond better to building a relationship by watching videos or are they going to be people who would rather read things or perhaps look at pictures?

People with different psychological ways and outlooks will have a different means of connecting. Some people like to see things; some people like to hear things, and some people like to touch things. So organising something like an investor day is a really good way of sharing what you're doing and talking through the processes that you go through so that it becomes very much a hands-on experience for people. Obviously, if you're just starting out, that's maybe a bit harder to do. But if you've got projects already, why not share that experience with other people by having open days and tours of properties? Or you can do that virtually with the use of video and just talk through the particular project. For example, I was with a client recently talking about creating almost an online journal using Facebook or LinkedIn. This could be just little snippets of where you were during a particular week and what property action you've taken and what you've achieved and what you've learned and how that was impacting on where you wanted to go in the future.

Making videos

Technology the way it is at the moment, it's very easy to shoot and promote videos of yourself. You just need to get the discipline to plan what you will say in the videos and set up the environment to actually do it – there's nothing difficult about it.

I did a short course with a guy who was a BBC TV filmmaker, and he worked on things like Teletubbies, and he said the quality of the camera in the latest smartphones is better than the broadcast quality they use at the BBC; so you know, there's kind of no excuse. You've got a film studio in your pocket. The smartphones today are extraordinary in what they can do, and it's worth experimenting and understanding what they are capable of doing. It's phenomenal, and few of us use it to its maximum capability.

Should you use ethical bribes?

Ethical bribes are taught in a lot of property seminars. An ethical bribe might be a lump sum of cash or a holiday in your apartment in Spain or an item of jewellery. But is this a good idea?

The topic of the ethical bribe – in my book, I know that some people suggest that it's part of the route of success, almost trampling on people just to get to where you want to get to at all costs, and that's not something that I subscribe to. I don't feel comfortable with it; it doesn't meet with my personal values, and I share the view very much of my property tax advisor, and he describes it beautifully. He describes a pack of wildebeests crossing the Savannah in Africa and the safety in numbers, and obviously the wildebeest right at the centre of the herd is pretty safe from predators, the lions, who will be circling the herd as they cross the Savannah. The point here is that if you are doing an undertaking of strategies and behaving in a way that puts you on the very edge of the boundaries of legality, you run the risk of being picked off. Now, that doesn't fit well with me. I would rather know that I was operating within the sort of legality, knowing there are those who will choose not to do that, but that's their choice and my choice. My reason to get involved with property is to provide for me and my family, and to risk that by taking, in my view, unnecessary steps is not a risk that I'm prepared to take. I do understand that some people perceive the need to do this, but actually, I think if you get the right strategy and you follow the right rules and ethics, there is no reason why you shouldn't make the kind of money that allows you to achieve the kind of goals that you're after. Why risk it for the sake of being unnecessarily risky in what you're doing?

And one of the sort of life experiences that I've had is that before I knew what I was doing, I invested in opportunities that appeared to be too good to be true and, without exception, they've all bitten me – and looking back retrospectively, I would've been better off taking a more conservative line and going for certainty rather than potentially risking everything. And, actually, over the longer term, taking those small steps tends to be the way forward for the vast majority. Now, I understand there will be people who will be wanting to take those risks; perhaps they're younger than I am, perhaps they've got less at stake, and it's worth them gambling with potential opportunities, but I believe it was Warren Buffett who said the first secret to making money is not to lose it, and the higher risk strategies including doing things that may be regarded as slightly off path to me are unnecessary risks that potentially might lead you to greater losses than perhaps the benefits in the longer term.

It's like asking your bank manager for a loan ...

I think there are a great many similarities between raising private finance and asking your bank manager for a loan. The whole business of doing your due diligence and understanding the numbers for any project will stand you in really good stead whether you're going to a bank manager, to a commercial lender, to a mortgage broker or to a private investor – the process is actually very similar, and the more you understand about how a private investor operates or how a bank operates, the more likely you are to achieve success.

I recently met a successful property investor from London who had developed a good relationship with a commercial lender. He understood the criteria that they were looking for, and by developing that relationship over a period of time, he was able to get better deals than your average property investor because he understood the criteria by which he was being judged. He presented his case in such a way that it ticked all the boxes. It's the same with a private investor. By understanding who your investors are, what their pain points are and how you're going to solve their problem, it's a very similar process. Obviously, with a bank or a mortgage lender, you've perhaps got a more structured approach for looking at it. In reality, very similar things are happening.

Lukewarm leads – when they're not yet ready

It's important to understand where people are in their process and be in alignment with what works for them. It may be that you say to somebody, "I haven't got a project live at this moment, but these are the kinds of projects that we're looking at. We'd like to be in a position to move quickly when we do find something that meets all of our criteria. In order for us to be able to move quickly, it would be useful to have cash available in the bank and ready to go." So you might reach some sort of agreement to hold that cash at a reduced rate of interest while you source an appropriate and suitable project. That's a negotiation between you and a potential investor to how you make that work.

Remain flexible and open to opportunity. There is no set way of doing it. The other alternative is just to have a wide pool of potential investors on tap so that if it doesn't suit one person at a particular time, maybe it suits somebody else. A lot of this is down to how much you actually need and when you may be needing it. If you need a total of £50,000, and someone offers it to you, might you take it a month or two earlier than you actually need to in order to secure it and take away the worry and the risk. It may be worth paying a couple of extra months' interest just to absolutely know you've got the money there and ready to go. Or, do you take a risk? It's different depending on each individual's situation. It's just personal judgement when it comes to that.

Keeping leads warm / social media / Staying in Touch

I frequently send out emails saying, "We've got opportunities, if you'd like more details let me know." Or, if you have got a project going through just share details with your personal network via email or social media. Share your story – it's all about planting your garden with flowers. If you've got stuff that's of interest, they – the butterflies -- will stay engaged. If you switch off communication and let the flowers die, they'll go.

Social media is brilliant because you can create a story – whether it's on a blog or a Facebook page. It's so easy to set up a really good website simply and cheaply these days. It doesn't really need to have fancy SEO; if you've got somewhere you can show how you've helped people and the kind of projects you've been involved with, that all helps to build a story, and it's easy to do. If you've been talking about walking the dog or going on holiday or going to a concert or something, you've got more than the connection of the property, the project, and the finance – those are really good things to add to the relationship.

For me, personally, when I'm sending out emails, when you are dealing with specific projects, it's much better to write personalised emails to a specific person. Rather than sending out a blanket email that's rather impersonal, I tend to take the time to create a more or less standard template but with the opportunity for putting in a couple of sentences that are specific to the person I'm addressing in that email. It just makes it that much more personal and engaging. It does take time, and I'm sure there are sophisticated systems to overcome that, but it's a cost time balance. It may be that you need to get somebody else to actually do the sending for you, but I find there's huge value in taking the time to engage properly with people rather than sending a rather anonymous templated email that's just very generic and has no personal value. I get that it's increasingly difficult to do when you're busy, but I frequently work my way through a database of about 3000 people and will send a personalised email to every single one of them.

I'm sure if you had a really good PA you could outsource this work, but for me, it's a personal relationship, and therefore, it's a bit like getting somebody else to take your wife out on a date night. What's the point of that, you know? Is that just me or is that insane?

Sealing the deal step by step

The first thing to do is to understand what the pain is that you're addressing. You then build that relationship so that the potential investor understands the process you go through when you're managing a project. You need to present the numbers and details of your project in a way that ticks the boxes of the investor.

Next, rather than saying, *"This is the rate of interest that we're prepared to offer,"* it's better to say to potential investors, "OK we've got this project, if you were to invest, what level of return would you consider attractive?" This way, two things are happening. One, you're not pushing anybody into anything; you're not pressuring them to invest. You're giving them the opportunity to come back and say, "Well, this is the level of interest that would be attractive to me." You might be surprised. I've had a couple of circumstances where I was prepared to offer a higher level of interest, and they came back and it was 6% lower. So, had I gone in and blurted what I was prepared to offer, it would have cost me more than if I had just kept my mouth shut and asked what they had been happy with. There is almost an expectation from people to think they've got to over-deliver on these things when that's frequently not the case. If investors have got the boxes ticked for what they're looking for, they may surprise you with how little interest they're prepared to accept comparative to what you may be expecting.

So, once you've done that, you've got to establish if it's a "go" situation; you've got to establish how readily available funds are. I've had situations where somebody said, "Well, that's great, I'd love to invest, we've got the money." We've agreed the interest rates, and you say, "OK, the project is ready to go now, when are funds available?" Only to discover they're locked into a 90- day account or a five-year bond, and they're not available to invest from a month to years, and that's a really important point. Just because somebody's got money, doesn't mean to say that it's available now. So you need to bring this question into the conversation to establish, "If this project was to go live next week, have you got funds ready to transfer, can we get them into the appropriate account in readiness for doing the deal?"

Then, it's a case of drawing up the necessary paperwork, getting the loan agreements signed and getting the money transferred over. There's no reason why it can't be a fairly straightforward process, once you've done the money laundering checks, of course. Make sure you know where the money is coming from.

Case Study 7

I had a man called Tom approach me because he was finding deals and was getting very frustrated because he was not able to find the finance. It was to do with how he was approaching the prospects. He was pushing people away rather than attracting them to him.

He was missing out steps in the relationship-building phase and expecting to be able to jump steps without going through the process properly. So he was building up greater and greater frustration, and in doing so, actually pushing people away harder and harder than ever before because he was coming across in entirely the wrong way. A little bit like networking, people are sort of thrusting a card into your hand and saying, "Make contact with me," without talking to you or without building a relationship and engaging with you.

In fact, if you were able to spin it round the other way and have somebody approach you in the same way, I'm sure you would see and understand the error of this approach. This is quite a frequent problem. The whole approach is wrong, and it's pushing people away rather than attracting them in. My whole process is about attracting people, not trying to press gang them or bully them, to give you money. It's a very calm and measured approach rather than jumping up and down and creating a big song and dance about it.

How to avoid a high-risk strategy

I think a high-risk strategy is anything that you don't fully understand and you don't understand the whole mechanics of how that particular project works. You could say that even a single buy-to-let property is high-risk if you don't know what you're doing. The more advanced the strategy, the greater the knowledge that you need in order to do that successfully.

You hear of people who particularly before "the crash" had

money in property. They were too highly geared, and when the market crashed, they lost everything, and they hadn't taken precautions to protect and preserve their wealth. So, anything that you don't fully understand falls into the category of "high risk", and that could be something as simple as a single buy-to-let. It might be HMOs if you don't understand HMOs; it might be serviced accommodation if you don't understand serviced accommodation. It could certainly be development if you don't understand development.

This is why training and education are so important. Learn from people who have that knowledge and experience, who perhaps made mistakes themselves and learned from them. They will have now got the systems in place to ensure that the work that they're doing is secured and that they understand what the risks are, and they can take the necessary steps to protect their investment. They can show you how to do the same thing and avoid the pitfalls that they might have fallen into.

Know your exit strategy

It's important to understand the system and the process that is involved when seeking property investment. When you go into any property field, it's essential to understand how you can exit that field. For example, if you're doing an HMO, your preferred option might be to find a property that is in need of refurbishment, adding value. It's not impossible to find below-market-value properties at the moment; however, in the current market, you're more likely to find opportunities where you can add value, so you might want to refinance it, keep the property and subsequently rent it out. But if for whatever reason that isn't an option, what are your other options? It's good to understand what those options are and being happy with your alternatives – and there might be three or four different alternatives.

So, one alternative might be to add the value and sell it; so, what are the implications of that? How long is that going to take to accomplish? Understand what your alternative options are so that you're protected, depending on what the market is doing. We've experienced a lot of uncertainty with 'Brexit' and the election in the USA, the election in the UK – we still don't really know where we're at. These things are going to be factors, but we have to recognise that external factors are going to affect what we're doing the whole time; you can only make judgements on what you're going to do based on what you know right now. You can't second guess things that may or may not happen because if you did, you'd never do anything. The point is to have multiple exits so that you're not stuck with something that doesn't work.

Think several moves ahead …

It's a bit like a game of chess: you're trying to think several moves ahead, but there are always going to be things that come along that you just can't account for. You're trying to hedge your bets the whole time. You're working out what the worst possible case is, being happy with that rather than the best possible case. Obviously, there are things you cannot necessarily control, but you do everything that's within your control to make sure your worst case scenario doesn't happen. But, as long as you're happy with the worst case, everything else that's better than that is a bonus. It's about mitigating your risks by understanding where and what those risks are. That's why it's important to do your due diligence properly so that you understand the full nature of what you're getting into.

Staying on the right side of the Financial Conduct Authority (FCA)

So, as far as the FCA goes, make sure that you have proper legal and property tax advice from a recognised professional. It's important to get your own professional advice and can make sure whatever strategy you're following falls within guidelines that you're happy and comfortable with and that you understand.

Choosing the right solicitor and accountant

A good solicitor is essential to your deal. The best thing to do is to make sure that the people you're working with have got experience in whatever documentation and proposals you're going through. There are people who will guide you with property-related legal matters.

The same sort of thing goes for choosing an accountant. Go about this exactly the same way as you'd go about choosing a solicitor. Everybody's tax position is different and unique to them, so it needs to be somebody who understands your position and what you're doing, and also has knowledge of property taxes. Property taxes are obviously quite different than general accounting. There are all sorts of laws and legislations that have been written into law quite recently that accountants need to be aware of, so a general High Street accountant is unlikely to be an appropriate solution.

There's a saying that goes something along the lines of: "If you think it's expensive to hire a professional, just see how much it costs to deal with an amateur." The cheaper option may seem like a good alternative, but it will help you more to get people who know what they're doing and how they're doing it. You may find that it takes several months longer to do things, and there may be costs attached to that.

It might be that there's a certain set of rules and regulations that you need to comply with that a professional will know about, and somebody who is not perhaps qualified or equipped to deal with that, you'll find yourself having to fight fires. So understanding what you're doing and how you're doing it is of critical importance, and understanding what your parameters are and what the expectations are. It comes back to service agreements and understanding what your expectations are all the way down the line for every element of it. Dotting i's and crossing t's and making sure you're comfortable with the process of what you're actually going to do.

There's a great phrase that I recall from my childhood, "An empty barrel makes most noise." Just because somebody is yelling and shouting about it doesn't make them an expert. It's often the quieter guy that is just getting on with it is the one you want to be dialling in to. Just because somebody is shouting from the rooftops -- why are they shouting from the rooftops? What inadequacies are they hiding? That's a bit of a broad generalization, but I remember my dad actually saying once, the longer the bonnet of the car, the bigger the car. It's perception of how people view others.

Processes to follow if things go wrong

The first thing to do is to look at what might go wrong, and typically the biggest challenge is that a project overruns and instead of taking 12 months, it takes 18 months. What do you do in that six-month gap? This is where the relationship with the investor is so important. You need to be talking to your investor the whole time, to keep them posted about what's happening and what the issues are. The quicker you can flag up issues, the better. You don't want to set alarm bells ringing, but to keep people informed. These sorts of conversations need to happen before you start working with investors. In the interest of transparency, you need to point out that there is risk attached to property, and what kinds of risks you may be exposed to: for example, it may be that the work will take longer or costs be more than expected.

Particularly at the moment, surveyors are down-valuing property prices in some areas so you might have done a refurbishment and expect to add £50,000 pounds to the value of the property, only to be looking for that value to refinance it to pull the finance out. Instead, that survey comes back in, and rather than increasing the value by £50,000, you only increase it by £20,000. There are areas you don't necessarily have control over like unforeseen building works or the valuation process. What are the implications for this for the investor? Are they still willing to accept the risks for the return they are getting? There are things you can do to mitigate those aspects, but ultimately, it's out of your control.

Speed and certainty ...

I think in a way, speed and certainty are combined. It's a benefit to vendors to know, particularly if you've got funds available: it puts you in a very strong position to negotiate property. One of the things that people who are looking to sell property look for is that speed and certainty, particularly if they are motivated sellers. So, it will put you in a good position if you are well armed with finance available to make quick purchases. Having great investors on board who understand this principle will help you in your endeavours.

How quickly can you access the cash?

I think particularly if you're working with investors, you're more likely to look at and secure the funds either in your own account or perhaps in a solicitor's ESCROW account so that the money is available to use at any given time.

One of the challenges that I've experienced myself is in being told by an investor that he had funds available and ready to go and then at 9 p.m. the night before exchanging on a property, that the account was withdrawn.

That was one of the very first deals that I was looking to get. It was with a joint venture partner; we sourced the property together, and I lined up a potential investor to put down funds for the deposit to allow us to actually go ahead and purchase it.

I remember getting the call at 9 p.m. on a Monday evening. We were due to exchange at 12 noon the following day. Being relatively inexperienced at that stage, I hadn't lined up an alternative. So it was that one investor or nothing. As it turned out, it was nothing. There was a change of circumstance over the weekend. I think a family member had been made redundant; I can't remember exactly, but I didn't blame the investor since there was nothing they could've done. But my heart just sank, and obviously I immediately lost face with the estate agent because they were of the understanding that we were ready to go, and as far as we were concerned, we were good to go. It would've been better for us to have actually secured the funds when they said the money was going to be available and taken the hit from the interest perspective just for the extra week or two to have had the funds in our pocket. But we didn't do that, and so the course of history was changed.

Avoid having all your eggs in one basket …

Until you've got a bird in the hand, as it were, it's best to keep on your toes. We were going looking for properties knowing we were going to buy; we knew roughly what project we were going to be looking for. This is why my teaching now is that people define their ideal deal so they know what the numbers are, and they can be prepared for all eventualities.

We were finding the deal and then trying to find the cash for it. We were relatively inexperienced at that time and didn't have a back-up of potential other investors to step in when our main investor pulled out. It was only £50,000, but having nine hours – well, we had about three working hours to find an alternative – it just wasn't enough. So, we lost face with the estate agent which ruled out us being able to comfortably go back to that agent again. Luckily, you don't have to work with every agent, but it did teach us a lesson to be more open and more transparent about how we were doing things. If you're working with estate agents, just keep them fully informed of what you are doing; don't try to be clever about it. We thought we were doing something really clever, and it bit us, so it kind of serves us right really. But we didn't know that at the time.

The importance of due diligence

Certainly when I was starting out, I was wide eyed and bushy tailed and willing to take on absolutely everything and anything that came my way without really considering the consequences of what I was getting into. I trusted other people more than I trusted myself at that stage, and I believed the stories that I was being told about their level of experience and what they'd done previously perhaps, without really doing my due diligence on the people I was working with. I think this is a real lesson of caution– just because someone says they're amazing, and just because there's social proof that supports that, really drill down and understand what questions you need them answering. I used to take people's words for what they were good at and didn't drill down deeply enough to understand where the gaps were in the processes that they were doing. My expectation was that they were probably better than they were, and the stories I was being told supported my thinking, so I blindly accepted it. That certainly didn't do me any favours really. Of course, it's easy to see with hindsight.

Crowd Funding

Crowd funding is definitely something to consider regarding raising private finance from armchair investors. There are a number of excellent property centric platforms out there. They operate on the basis of attracting finance from a large group of smaller investors to fund a single property project. Whilst there are limitations and restrictions to this form of funding, I would certainly recommend exploring the possibilities. All of the same principles apply to this as for finding your own armchair investors. You will need to convince the platform that you have a viable project to fund and that you have done proper due diligence. This may not be for you if you are just starting out as they will usually require a track record of delivering projects on time and to a budget.

Explore this as an option though to add to your armoury of different solutions.

Stress and how to cope with it.

I think the first thing to recognise is that it's not *if* stress happens, it's *when* it happens. In any business, you need to expect these things rather than discover, "Oh my goodness, I'm having a stressful day." One of the speakers at an event I attended recently is a hugely successful property investor. In his first opening words, he said: "I've had a rough day, a very challenging day, and it's quite a relief to come out and talk to you so I can distract myself from all of those challenges." The important thing is to recognise that it's to be expected, and it's normal. So, having a strategy to be able to deal with that is hugely important.

I start my day with a half-hour walk that just gets in oxygen and gets the blood circulating. I try, particularly when the business day is really hectic, to just take five-minute sessions to go out of the office environment and sit quietly in a quiet space and just focus on breathing. It's very basic meditation; just clearing your mind of everything. We have, I think, 50-60,000 thoughts a day; it's an insane amount, and to just focus on your breath allows you to acknowledge thoughts and then go back to focusing on your breath. There are lots of different styles of meditation and podcasts, books, classes you can go to and learn more about meditation. It really is powerful. Just make some clear space; space allows you to create a vacuum and allows things to come into the mind. If you're constantly active, you're not giving sufficient space to allow that to happen. Space can help you to overcome stressful situations.

I have experimented with many types of alternative therapies. Including homeopathy, Network Spinal Analysis (NSA) with Somato Respiratory Integration (SRI), and Pilates. Massages are another really good way of de-stressing. I'm currently experimenting with Ayurvedic massage, which is combined with Indian herbs. It's an ancient healing process that allows your energy to flow more effectively around your body and allows your body to heal itself. I think it comes with eating appropriately and giving your body the right fuel to power through the pain and deal with stress more effectively.

Be conscious of what you're eating; if you're putting trash and fast food into your body, you can't expect your thoughts and actions to be as good. If you put substandard fuel into a car, it's going to misfire; it's no different for humans. We are very intricate machines, and whilst there is a certain amount of tolerance, if you keep putting the wrong fuel in, you're never going to get the best results.

I think also that reading can help some people because you're focusing on the text that you're looking at. Music is a great calming influence for others. It depends on the type of music you're listening to. Clearly, upbeat music isn't going to do anything to calm you down, though it may lift your spirits. Or something different may be an appropriate thing that works for you. The point is to help calm you when you experience stress levels going up, so you can kick into action very quickly and not get overwhelmed. Having been there, in a very big way in the stress and depression department, I can tell you that it's not good for your long-term health at all. It's better to manage it at the source than go with it once it's long-term. Recognise that you can choose what you eat and how you feel. Why would you choose anything other than the best?

Recovering from challenges

Sometimes, it's a case of just getting back on your horse and dusting yourself off.

I think it's recognizing and being brave and courageous enough to understand that perhaps you haven't made the best decision you could have. If I look back, some of the decisions that I've made were the best that I could have made at the time that I made them. It's only in retrospect that they didn't turn out to be the best decisions. But given the circumstances that I was in at the time, I didn't appear to have much by way of choice. Actually, you do always have a choice and the time to do things properly. Take that time, and if necessary, get professional guidance to help you.

Tips for self-care

For example, it might be going for a massage, going for a walk, going sailing, doing things that lift your spirits.

I think it is important to recognise that we are human and that we all make mistakes from time to time. You can only do at any one moment in any day what seems to be the most appropriate thing at that time. You must, therefore, look after yourself and put yourself as number one. It's the classic airline story that when the oxygen masks come down, you need to make sure that you look after yourself first so that you're then in a position to look after others.

When you recognise you're not in perhaps the place that you want to be, what support is available and what action can you take to recover? The first thing is recognizing that you're not in the place that you wanted to be in. Acknowledging that is the first step to recovery for problems, and once you acknowledge that, you're then open to potential support and making progress in resolving those issues – whatever those issues may be that you've found yourself confronting.

Creating peak performance

Self-care is essential in maintaining peak performance. This means things like getting enough sleep, eating the right foods, protecting yourself from toxic and negative people around you.

I think it's important to find a routine and a system that works for you. We're all busy people, and if you immerse yourself in property, and particularly if you're working as well as trying to do property, you'll find that time is something that really needs to be valued. You really need to closely look at how you're investing your time, and unless you take care of yourself both physically and mentally, you won't be able to cope and deal with situations as they arise.

Firstly, this involves eating healthily. For myself, I try to avoid processed foods, and I've cut out caffeine, and I've tried to cut down on sugar – things that we know are detrimental to health in modern life. Prepared food contains all sorts of additives and extras that we don't actually need, but the sort of convenience style of living tends to promote these things, and it's just a case of planning better. Planning your week in advance and making sure you've got fresh food available to eat and to be able to feed your mind as you go through the week. If you're skipping meals and you're eating bad food, it's a bit like putting petrol into a diesel car. If you're not putting the right fuel in, you wouldn't expect the vehicle to go anywhere, and it's the same with us. We are very, very intricate, mechanical machines.

Secondly, aim to drink the right amount of water; I aim to drink at least two litres of water a day. I have a fairly high protein-rich diet and also try to eat salads and lots of greens every day. I don't have anything like a perfect diet, but I work towards that incrementally.

Someone once said to me, "If you eat a salad one day, are you going to be healthy any more than if you eat a burger and chips, are you going to be unhealthy?" It's not the one-off, it's the period of let's say a year. If somebody eats a burger and chips every day for 12 months, there's going to be a difference in their body compared to somebody who has eaten healthy salads and less processed foods. Over that period of time, you're going to see a marked difference to energy levels, to quality of thought, to general well-being. It allows you to be more resistant to infection, allowing you to fight off disease. I don't pretend to be a doctor or a medic in any way, but I have coaches and advisors that help me on health because for me health is critical and without it you simply can't function properly and expect to be at your best.

I've heard stories about the Formula 1 motor racing world, and they're spending millions and millions of pounds developing the cars and getting the cars to be absolutely spot on, and they suddenly realised that one of the key things that was most variable was the driver. Making sure that the driver was at absolute peak was a critical element of that; any sportsman is only as good as the food that they eat and the training that they do.

Why is it any different from sports to business to property? So, being mindful of what we eat, what we drink – I'm certainly not proclaiming to be perfect on any of these, but certainly more mindful of it; taking time out to perhaps reflect, meditate, focus on breathing, just simple things. Also, exercise and walking – again I'm not perfect by any stretch – but I just try to keep in good physical shape, and certainly in the last five or six years I've seen a marked improvement in my personal health. I used to get sick very quickly, very easily. I was always prone to catching colds, and being a father with four children coming back from school they were continually suffering colds, and I would be the first to catch those. Now, I'm the last person in the family, usually, to catch anything. That's been hard work to turn around. Just be conscious of these things.

A good daily routine works wonders

My morning involves getting up, and the first thing I do is make sure I'm hydrated, so I usually have a glass of water by my bed. Then, I'll have a cup of green tea infused with half a fresh lemon and a couple of slices of root ginger. I'll then go for usually half an hour or so for a brisk walk; sometimes with the dog, sometimes not depending on who else is available to walk the dog. That will be followed by a protein at breakfast like a protein smoothie or scrambled eggs. Midway through the morning, I'll have an apple usually with some peanut butter, and lunch is normally fish salad; ideally, I'd have fresh fish, but that's not always possible, so I'll have sardines or mackerel with a green leaf salad.

By mid-afternoon, I'll probably have a seed bar, and in the evening I'll have some chicken along with some vegetables. I normally mix them all into one pot, and that's usually a combination of onion, chicken, perhaps pork, vegetables, tomatoes – a kind of chowder out of what's available in the fridge. I try and drink at least two litres of water a day and probably have a couple of green teas throughout the day as well. I'll supplement that with a couple of multivitamins and other things just to help with joint pain. And that's it – pretty typical.

If I'm out and about, I'll try and fit in with that same routine as best as I can. If I were better planned, I'd prepare food for the week to take it with me, but I still have to work on that. I'm not Captain Perfect by any stretch of the imagination. I try and do some sort of a workout, but it's all bodyweight stuff, and I try and get a full 10,000 paces a day which is sometimes difficult in a busy week. But rather than beating yourself up for not achieving it in one day, try and have an average of 10,000 paces over a seven-day period. Over the weekend or in the evening, I might go for a longer walk just to play catch up on days that I had more to do at work. So it's things you can do wherever you are.

Case Study 8

I've had a man in the office who, on the face of it, was very successful. He had got 30 rooms under management as HMOs and was doing really well. But again, he just had the barriers that were stopping him that he felt uncomfortable asking for money.

He'd always been very independent in terms of being self-supporting, very conservative in his approach as to how he tackled things. Therefore, he didn't really like the idea of working with other people. He'd never worked in sales, so he perceived this whole process as being a sales process, and he also had very strong ethics. He wanted to make sure that he knew how he could repay people and pay people. So I helped him to address all of those concerns because they're not just concerns of the borrower, they're also concerns of the lender, and this is about understanding how both parties can benefit.

So the value that I gave was by changing his perceptions and digging deep into why he perceived these particular things to be such big blocks, and I helped him to overcome the need to know that he can repay people. It's about understanding the numbers, being really clear about what the numbers are before you start approaching people, and being clear in your own mind, for your own peace of mind, to be able to understand the whole process so that when you go into a project, you're absolutely confident that it is going to be successful and that you are going to be able to come out of it well.

This one chap was hugely experienced and a very good project manager, but he still held these fears that he wasn't going to be able to repay the investor. These are the core things you need to be addressing right at the front and to have multiple exit strategies.

Quite often, I talk to people, and they've only got a single exit strategy for a project. They go in thinking, "We are going to do X," and their focus is on achieving that, which is great, but they have no alternatives. It's important to have more than one exit strategy that you're comfortable with that will work properly. Quite often people overlook that. They're not prepared enough to be able to answer questions such as, "What if the best thing doesn't happen?" "Where are you going to go if that ceases to be an option for you?" They haven't considered the options that are available to them at the front end.

If you know what your options are, and you're happy with the worst-case scenario, you then do everything in your power to make sure that the worst doesn't happen, and everything that you achieve above that is a bonus. The way that most people look at this is, "We want the best thing to happen, and, oh my goodness, if anything other than this happens then we're stuck."

Again, it's just changing the way that you look at things very slightly and looking at it from the worst-case scenario rather than the best case. That way, you're protecting both yourself and your investor to make sure that you're covered on the project.

My client decided to go ahead and implement my changes and suggestions. The impact will be that the goals that he wants to achieve become achievable very much quicker because he's able to create case studies to attract people in and know with confidence that the action that he's taking will get him results and move him forward. There is always a little nervousness to start, and that's understandable because quite frequently you're changing beliefs that you've held perhaps for your whole life.

I understand that, because of my own personal beliefs and my own personal challenges, that you don't necessarily change those overnight. It's a progression. You need to see the results happening in order to have the confidence to keep going. It's about trusting the process and understanding that if you do keep going, you will start to see the results. But if you keep doing the same things, you're going to keep getting the same results that you always have. So it's trusting the process and understanding that the road will come up to meet you as you take those next steps.

But I'm there to provide the support and the guidance and to help him understand that process and that it is valid. To help him understand the reactions and the responses he gets from the people that he's working with so that when he does start to see change, he recognises that change is in the right direction, and that it is positive, and that it is progress towards him achieving his results.

So, a lot of it's about understanding that there is a process and there is a system, and that with guidance and help, you can effect this change. So often, people are so much closer than they realise to striking gold, but because they haven't experienced this themselves, they can't see where they are in the process, and they can't see how close they are. And I guess it's that experience that I bring to it that I can see where they are on their journey and to know where to shine the light in order that they can take the next step.

Keeping track of everything that you do

In the course of a week, you can have multiple phone calls, and you can meet a lot of people. It's therefore important to keep track of everything you've said and everyone you've spoken to.

Personally, I have a contact management system that I record against each contact; their full contact details and then I make notes of anything I've said. If I've made notes, I will scan them in because I'm not good at organizing paper; I'm better at organizing it on a computer because you can create files and folders. So, a number of my investor files are there so I know where they are, and I'm not hunting around for them. I just attach all of my notes to the contact file.

I also try to create task lists to keep in touch with the people that I need to keep in touch with. I'm not the best at this; I have to admit, I could be better. I tend to write things down in a diary; I'm not an electronic wizard. If I'm not very, very organized, I can lose the information by misnaming the file or creating a different file. So I need to be extremely disciplined in the whole process. If you find that this isn't something that comes naturally to you, perhaps you need to be looking at some point in the not too distant future to actually get help in that area to organize your schedule for the week.

I tend to plan my week in advance, so on a Sunday evening I'll sit down and plan what I'm hoping to achieve during the week so that I'm not having to think it up every day. I'll have one core thing that I'm meant to focus on that particular week, and that might be to find investors, to find new clients; it might be working on the book, something that I actually want to achieve during the course of that week. By having a goal, I can then figure out what steps I need to take in order to achieve the goal. I think by writing it down, it brings it to life. If it's just in your head, you run the risk of forgetting. Writing it down has a very powerful effect.

Getting personal ...

If someone tells you what their hobbies are or a little about their private life, keep a note of this so that when you reconnect you can remember to ask them about it, say if they've been in a tennis championships recently, so that you're not just focusing only on the deal but also building a relationship with them.

Anything that can expand your engagement with somebody is always good. Just talking business all the time can be quite limiting, so having a broader interest in somebody is massively helpful. It shows interest and goes back to something I said earlier in the book: that to be interesting you need to be interested. Just show an interest, perhaps not in everything that they do but pick out one or two things that maybe resonate with you and help to build that relationship.

Define your big reason *why*?

Have a big reason *why* you are doing everything. When you're investing in property, in general, there are going to be moments when things aren't necessarily going how you'd like. So the *why* that is the motivation for you has to be huge. Understanding *why* you're doing something and what achieving that particular goal would mean to you is something that you can dial into in those darker moments when perhaps things aren't going according to plan. You should be able to draw strength from it.

You hear some amazing stories of people who've got children with disabilities or illnesses that they're trying to overcome; people who do amazing charity work; it needs to be something that resonates with you. It's really important that it's *your* reason why and not somebody else's. So, just because somebody else is driven by wanting to help a child or a family member, perhaps. It's important that it's *your* reason why. Very often a stronger reason *why* will be something that you do for somebody else rather than something for you. Often that's a more powerful reason for getting you out of bed and getting you to take action, and it's a tough decision to be made. Particularly when you've got an awkward call to make or a situation that's more than we'd normally be comfortable with, but if your *why* is bigger than that fear, that will help you to get through that moment.

Big reasons why

There's one guy who has got a disabled son; he is in a wheelchair. His son asked one day why he wasn't able to play football like all his friends, and his dad didn't have an answer to that. So he was massively motivated to get property to be able to finance and fund the creation of a wheelchair football team, which became a reality because he was so clearly focused on achieving that. That's a pretty massive why. Often why's that are created for somebody else are more powerful than why's for yourself.

Let's say, for example, you have a family, and your reason why was to take them on a family holiday of a lifetime, perhaps to America or Europe or wherever it might be. You put it out there to your family that is what you're going to do, so there's an awful lot of pressure on you to then achieve that goal, whereas if you haven't created accountability, it may be easy to shuffle under the carpet and forget your goal. So, making your why public can be very powerful. Some people are more private about it, and that's fine; it's whatever works for you. But frequently, the big why is to do with some sort of charity or helping people in the Third World. One person I know has set up homes for victims of domestic abuse, and they wanted to create a special environment for them, instead of dregs style accommodation. So they were using their property knowledge and expertise for good social benefit to create something that answered a problem. In fact, I know a number of friends who have set up housing projects and put their property knowledge to really good use in helping aspects of society that may not have otherwise received support.

It's tempting but ...

Red flags can appear as inconsistencies in people's stories; where they say they're going to do something and don't meet their promises, or you notice that they're exaggerating or telling lies.

One of the biggest things that is a red flag to me is people who say they are going to do something and don't, as I'm a very "instant" sort of person. I recognise that everybody's list of priorities isn't necessarily mine, but if there's an agreement to do something, I struggle with the concept of people not doing things that they've said they are going to do. That's a personal thing. In terms of other red flags, people may do something that's contrary to your values. Again, it's important to understand what your values are because if you understand where your values lie, you'll understand better when somebody breaks those values.

It goes back to understanding what makes us unique and seeing everyone else is unique as well. Everyone is going to have their own drivers and their own reasons for wanting to do what they do, and people can change when there is a large sum of money involved. Of course, property is very much about money and large sums of it, and sometimes people's total psyche changes when they get into close proximity to this, and that's something to be aware of. Some people can turn almost into a Jekyll and Hyde type character where they portray one image, but actually, they have a flaw almost that they don't necessarily perform in the same way or at the time in a consistent manner that's congruent with whatever the situation might be.

How do you ensure confidentiality?

I think sometimes people get carried away, and they don't necessarily realise they're breaking confidentiality and, again, it's understanding where people are in their lives. What pains and what drivers are working for them? We've all got other stuff going on in our lives, and that can influence and dictate sometimes how we behave, and it's not necessarily the real us that's in that situation. But it's the straw that broke the camel's back isn't it? You've got an underlying challenge; there may be something going on at home; you've got out of bed the wrong side, and your whole rationale goes out the window. I think it's important to recognise that you can do that but also other people may be going through exactly that, and the responses they give at a given time to a given situation may be something that they haven't thought about rationally. They just blurt something out without really understanding what they're doing or what they're saying because of how they are and what's happened to them and where they are in their journey at that particular time. You've got to be aware of it.

Should you sign a Non-Disclosure Agreement (NDA)?

I think it depends a little bit on the personal situation that you find yourself in and what you're comfortable with. There's no right or wrong here. It's taking a particular situation and understanding what the implications of where you are, what you're doing and the consequences of somebody not maintaining confidentiality – is that something that needs protecting or not?

This is a question you perhaps need to ask yourself when you enter into any specific agreement. Clearly, if I was working with investors, I'm not really going to talk about those people and their particular personal situation with other people. It's not ethical in my book. Sometimes that can be challenging, and you've just got to know where to draw the line.

Tips for overcoming nerves

You can sometimes experience nerves when you're talking with investors. The best way to overcome these nerves is to build your confidence based on facts. So, by understanding what the facts are of a particular situation, it will help you to build your confidence.

One of the things that I hear people get nervous about is just approaching an investor in the first instance and the whole hesitation around borrowing money from people. But, in fact, if you've done everything by the book and understood what a particular project involves and you've done all your due diligence properly, and the investor understands that, then you've done all you can. As long as you've been transparent with it, there shouldn't be any particular reason to be fearful or nervous. I think the nerves come to people when they're not sure that they've done their due diligence properly to be able to take it confidently to an investor or even trust their own judgement. That's where the real risks lie.

If you're not confident when you have done appropriate due diligence, it begs the question then *why* are you doing it? What support do you need in order to be able to turn this around? Perhaps the answer lies within a power team or getting help to address the issues that you're not comfortable or confident with. In my experience, the only reason for nerves is when you don't know what the outcome is. Sometimes it's OK not to know; it's OK to say "I need to get clarification on that point" or "Help me to understand more of what you're looking for," and those sorts of responses are absolutely fine because you're not expected to know everything all of the time, and it's just acknowledging that.

Look at the upside *and* the downside ...

Sometimes it's not easy to exit a particular deal, and this is why it's so important to understand going into a deal what the possible exits are and what the expectations of both sides are. Also, to understand what the service level agreements are between the various parties so that if any of those elements are breached, you can feel comfortable. You may need to get legal documentation to protect yourself. So often, particularly with joint ventures, people go in having only looked at the upside, and they haven't looked at all at the downside, and a huge number of joint ventures fall apart because people haven't examined the "what-ifs" regarding things going wrong. I advocate just working with loan agreements because they're much simpler documentation; it's a more straightforward relationship in terms of working with somebody because everything is absolutely clear: it's all in black and white. The simplicity is in the agreement. You are borrowing a fixed amount for a fixed term for an agreed rate of interest. There's no room for interpretation because there is nothing to interpret. If you get into a joint venture, you're opening up the possibility of misinterpretation because a standard JV is simply a blank sheet of paper, and while things are all nice and rosy, people see things differently. And it's not until things start to go wrong that people's perception of what was agreed changes. The longer and more complex the JV agreement is, the greater the opportunity for someone to pick a hole in it. I understand of course that JV's definitely have their place for the right people and the right project.

I think it's testament to the fact that so many joint ventures don't work out because that process hasn't been gone into. I, personally, don't advocate joint ventures at all, but if you do find yourself getting into a joint venture, you need to have a separate discussion completely aside from any deals that say, "OK, what do we do if things don't work out? What is the protocol that we follow when the proverbial hits the fan? How do we manage that process?"

It's a bit like having a complaints procedure in place before you actually tackle and join forces with somebody. Like I said previously in this book, if you're working with people who aren't good with money, they can go out of their heads when they see the possibilities and leave their rational brains behind. I've seen it so many times. They just look at the rosy side and don't look at the downside.

When you have to exit a deal

My personal recommendation is to talk to people rather than email because emails can be misconstrued and misinterpreted; particularly where there is tension, they will read something different than what was intended or than what appears to have been written. This is true of any documentation; people will interpret it in completely different ways depending on their perspective at the time of when something was presented. It's really important to understand that just because something is written down doesn't mean to say that understanding of that document is the same; everybody is unique and different, and they all have their very different viewpoints on what a particular circumstance is.

You've only got to read or listen to the news, and having been in the printing industry one of the first things we were taught was: the nearer you are to the news, the further it seems from the truth. When you read or hear it reported, you kind of question if you were at the same event which then brings into question if things you were witness to aren't being reported correctly. Whatever makes you think that the rest of what you're reading or listening to is any different? Reading a newspaper article or listening to someone on the TV is simply one person's perspective; it's their view of where they happen to be at that particular time, and it's nothing more than that. The same is true in life as well; it's somebody's understanding at a different angle to you; everyone has a different perspective, a different vision and view of what has been said. Very profound.

What about hospitality?

When building a relationship, hospitality is like the icing on the cake. A lot of big corporates know this – they'll take people out to horse racing, sailing, or send them chocolates or wine at Christmas. Hospitality can be used to enhance or build relationships.

I think it's important that every relationship will be different, and it's about understanding what the other person is looking for in a particular relationship – it's the PR aspect of setting up a deal. I call these "The Four Ps": we've got the people, the project, the paperwork, and the PR. Looking after the relationship is really key; understanding what makes investors tick. There's going to be a different way of doing that for each individual; so what works for one is not necessarily going to be congruent for other people, and just nurturing that relationship, just understanding why somebody is involved in that relationship will help you to gauge the most appropriate way of treating it.

I know a number of property people who have Investor Days where they invite their investors along to view a project, and there are some hospitality elements to that where they are answering questions but also offering some sort of food and drinks. It's about what people feel comfortable with and what their situation is as to what is going to work best.

The Four Ps:

- The people,

- The project,

- The paperwork

- The PR.

Some people choose to send gifts or take investors out to dinner. I think it's dependent on the relationship. It's nice to acknowledge people and their contributions and the things they've made and what they've done, but I think each individual needs to be treated individually. I don't think there's any one answer here really.

I don't think it's something obligatory; I think it depends on how the relationship is, and I would play it completely by ear. I think it's what works for you and what you're comfortable with.

Investor days

Investor days involve showing people what you're doing and just being open to answering questions. It's a word that we've used a lot – transparency – investors like to see what you're doing, talking about challenges you've experienced on a particular project, how you've addressed those challenges, how you work with your team – teams are very important, and no one expects you to do it all yourself. Sharing that you have a team and how you work with that team is important. It's just a really good opportunity to talk about concerns, and a little bit like the networking meetings; the good stuff comes out two or three hours after you've covered the basics and you start digging down into the deeper details. It's about building relationships and being open to the possibilities.

> ## Case Study 9
>
> One of my clients was venturing into buying their first HMO. They had previously had rental property but hadn't started stepping things up until they came to me. They had gone to get some quotes for this particular project, and they had sensibly shared their results with me. Looking at the paperwork, I was confident that I could help them find a better solution. I connected them to another broker who took the time and trouble to meet with the client and really understand what was required. The result was an astonishing saving of over £11,000 over six months, in interest and fees, by making sure they had the right product. That's a very significant saving and demonstrates the value of having access to the right people and resources.

Hosting your own networking events

There are benefits to hosting your own event rather than perhaps going to somebody else's networking meeting. So this is something you may wish to consider.

The big benefit of starting your own group is that you then become the authority – or perceived authority – because you're the figurehead. I'm lucky that I still benefit from having run a property meeting in the past. I still get asked if I still run the meeting when it's been nearly two years since I've stopped. The fact that I had run that meeting gives the perception that I am somebody who stepped up.

I'm also part of a small group that was set up a couple of months ago, and I think there are something like 50 members now. We meet once a month for an informal supper and chat about property issues. Usually, there is somebody who is sharing a little bit of knowledge or information which they specialise in. The guy who set it up is now the go-to person for connecting all of the people in that group; he's not a particularly experienced property investor himself; in fact, quite the reverse. But he's using the power of that group to help him achieve what he wants to achieve. He started the event as a meet-up group, but now it's gone on to be more of a Facebook group, but the physical meeting is once a month. It's very informal – in a pub or hotel, and we all pay for our own food – and it's just a great way of meeting people, building relationships. If you are the one who set that up, it gives you credibility; it gives you authority, and members will then want to come to you. Off the back of this, I have also set up a group, and one of the other members has also set up a group in our respective areas. Be a creator not a waiter, go out and create the environment you need to succeed.

The benefits of hosting your own events

I used to host a property event in Swindon. The benefit to me of running that was that it put my head above the crowd. All of a sudden, you're somebody that's being noticed. My picture was associated with the meeting in the back of the trade property magazines so people got to know who I was. It was building credibility, and it allowed me also to connect more effectively with people who are on the speaker circuit, so I now know a lot of good people who are sharing their knowledge and wisdom. It also got me to meet up with the 50 or so other hosts of other property groups. So it was useful to network with other people who were also in an elevated position. People came to you because of who you were. You were the one who knew everybody in the room and, therefore, you were in a position to help people and connect people.

I hosted the event for two years. I have continued to tell people that I've hosted it, so the perception is still there that I am confident enough to host a meeting. Part of all of this is telling everybody what you do, in whatever form you feel comfortable. The more people that get to see and hear your message, the better.

Is it OK to mix business with pleasure?

Again, I don't think there's a right or a wrong here. I wouldn't say, "Don't do it." I'd just say, "You need to be cautious of how things like that do develop, and use your own caution and values to assign whether something is appropriate or not." There may be situations where you're building a stronger bond, and that's completely appropriate, and there may equally be situations where it's completely inappropriate.

The beauty of a loan agreement

Sometimes you will have to structure more complex deals, but generally, my advice is to have a straightforward loan agreement, especially when you are getting started.

If you are doing something complex, then obviously a simple loan agreement may not be appropriate for that particular deal.

Absolutely seek proper professional advice from somebody who is acting on behalf of both you and the other side. It's important that both sides get proper professional advice on these things and that you don't get tempted to just say, "Oh well, it's a gentlemen's agreement." These things can and do take on a life of their own sometimes. It's not something you can really just leave to chance. I think one of the key things here is to remember that the cost of trying to repair something once it's broken is significantly higher than making it right in the first instance. Property projects can and do go wrong – that's kind of a fact of life. It's easier to put processes in place *before* they go wrong to know what to do when they do go wrong, not if, rather than wait till something's gone wrong and then try to figure out how you're going to pay for it and deal with it.

I think people sometimes fall into a "gentlemen's agreement" without necessarily intending to – because the paperwork supporting the agreement is little more than that. It may not be intentional, but it's kind of where they've left themselves exposed, and because they haven't got a comprehensive enough agreement in place, particularly if they're doing a joint venture, to cover all eventualities.

Loan agreements are very much simpler and more straightforward because they simply outline how much money is involved, what the interest is, how long the loan is for, and how it's going to be repaid. It's a very simple agreement. When you start going into joint ventures, you're starting with a blank sheet of paper asking both sides to say what it looks like and getting it drawn up legally, and it's open to interpretation.

100% interest rate that was too good to be true.

A client came in, a very seasoned professional property investor – he was very keen to see wealth generated for his investors and had a potentially great way of achieving that. But the way it was presented was such that my almost immediate reaction was to pull back because it sounded cheesy; it sounded too good to be true. He was offering something like 100% return, plus their original investment back, which was more like 200% interest rate.

So, here is what a private investor is likely to be thinking: "Help me to understand how that is possible!" You need to understand what people's expectations are because that preconditioning is likely to be for significantly lower rates of return. If you could achieve 100% to 200% normally with investments, why wouldn't everybody be doubling their money every year? If it was that easy, why wouldn't everybody be doing it all of the time? "Why am I being singled out for special treatment? What are the catches? Why am I being offered this? It's just too good to be true."

Even if somebody takes the time to explain it to me, I don't know that I'd trust it because I don't know how it's possible to do that when everyone else is offering maybe 10% or even less than that. How is somebody suddenly able to come along and offer hundreds of percentage points of interest? So, I think you need to be very careful about the messages that you send out. It may be a totally authentic and honest process, but actually, you're frightening people away by offering such huge rates of return because it's way outside of their comfort zone. There's just going to be that nagging little voice in the back of your head saying, "I'm not sure about this." If you're looking to attract people in, you've got to look at the message and put yourself in the shoes of the property investor – how are they going to perceive that? Is that really the message you want to be sending out?

The top fear of private investors

The biggest fear tends to be security. If I give you my money, what guarantee can you give me that I'm ever going to see it again? That's without question the biggest concern because over and above interest rates and anything else, they want to make sure they're not going to lose what they've given you, and that's an absolute priority.

There are things that you can do to offer that security. You need to explore what options you are prepared to offer and are able to offer to potential investors with you.

I think that's the biggest fear: the fear that you're just going to get up and go and never be seen again – but that's tied in with "How do I secure my investment?" "What's giving me comfort that you're going to do what you say you're going to do?" and

"How can I trust you to do that?"

I'd say without question the biggest voiced fear is that they're worried about being taken for a ride because it may be something they're not 100% familiar with. They may not be familiar with property as a proposition, so they're very heavily reliant on you, your knowledge, and your team to be able to deliver. Displaying credibility is huge, and it's part of building that relationship and gaining the trust.

How can you show that you're trustworthy?

Reassurance comes in different forms, and different investors will want different levels of assurance and reassurance. There are some investors who will request a charge against either the property that you're working on or another property. Now, some people will only invest with a first charge; however, if you've got a mortgage on the property, you won't be able to offer anybody else a first charge because the lender will want that.

It is usually possible to do a second charge on the property, and you can also do what's called "a restriction" (RX1). There are different options as far as security is concerned. You can also draw up loan agreements, personal guarantees, deeds of trust, etc. Again, you need to have professional advice on how to implement each and any of these options to make sure both parties are protected. If you do these things through solicitors and through indemnified professionals, you are making big strides in allaying fears. You can also encourage the other side to get proper advisors, and you may offer to pick up that bill.

OPPORTUNITY IS NOWHERE

Some people are frightened if you're sharing something that looks uncomfortable to them. We tend to take aim and fire at people who are doing something that is not in our framework. It's kind of built into our psyche now; we think it's normal and acceptable. Rather than saying, "Well done, I'd like a piece of that," people can be quite detrimental. That's their opinion, just be aware of it. Everything will always be just out of reach for those people because that's how they see the world.

One of the things that I use when I give talks is to ask my audience to write out "o-p-p-o-r-t-u-n-i-t-y-i-s-n-o-w-h-e-r-e". I then ask people what they see. Some people will see opportunity is "nowhere" and other people will see opportunity is "now here". Same letters, but different people see different things.

How to create an accurate cash flow forecast

This is why it's a great idea to work with a team and get in a project manager who understands this process. You need this for your own piece of mind, never mind the investors. If you don't understand these numbers and don't trust yourself on them, why would an investor? Yes, it's scary, but if it's scary, then find somebody who understands how these things work and make them part of your team. It's much cheaper to have somebody on your team who understands and can help manage and monitor that process as you go through it than it is to pay to pick up the pieces at the end. It can be quite expensive, particularly if you're borrowing hundreds of thousands of pounds. For example, at one point in my career, I had my name against about £1.5 million worth of leverage from investors. It's important that there are appropriate controls in place when handling this amount of finance.

It's not about plucking figures out of thin air; it's about having a team that has experience in these projects and can help you come up with realistic figures. Anybody who has managed a property project will know that you have to put contingency in there; you build contingency into pay the what-ifs. What if this happens, what is the impact of that?

One of my clients is a project manager who has worked on the Olympic Park in London and other big projects; he has to understand what if something doesn't happen when it's predicted to happen and what's the likely impact? You need to be on top of this the whole time. This is the world of a project manager – to keep their eye on where things are, how they're going, and it's choosing what's appropriate to feed back from that to your investors. Is it something you can manage, or do you need to highlight it? How serious is it? What are the implications? Property projects can and do regularly fall out of bed. The better managed they are, the more likely they are to stay on track.

Having the right team in place to help you achieve that is worth its weight in gold – particularly if it is a sizable project. If it is a smaller project, and you have built in plenty of time into your projections, maybe you don't need a project manager. But for a decent-sized project, you've got to have people who know what they're doing. You need to assess what level that team needs to be at for the nature of the project. Bringing a project home on time or having it overrun six months can have a massive impact on the amount of interest you pay. That could be the difference between a project making a profit or losing money. So, you need to have gone through that ahead of doing the deal to get yourself comfortable with the implications.

The grace period – why it's important for investors to know, like, and trust you

I think there's an element that if your investors know they can trust you, there might be some element of flexibility. I think if you're transparent about the whole process, you're more likely to get some sort of understanding than you are if you're very elusive and trying to cover things up. If people can see what's happening, they are more likely to be open to options and possibilities; it's when people are kept out of the loop and not informed that they start jumping to conclusions and making rash judgements. This can mean you are given a "grace period" when you overrun, for example, or when things don't go according to plan.

Factoring in safety nets

I've had at least one deal where I had an investor lined up and they were good to go, but we got a call at 9 p.m. on a Monday evening when we were due to exchange at lunchtime next day. They pulled out –- not because they were trying to be nasty to us, but because they had a change of circumstances, and it wasn't appropriate for them to lend the money.

It was one of the very, very early deals that I was involved in, and I didn't have a sufficient network at the time to be able to tap into any other resources. So, I think being aware of what your options are and what you can tap into is good. If you've got someone that is really reliable – maybe a family member – it's good to have somebody waiting in the wings should Investor 1 pull out.

The other challenge that you get quite frequently is that somebody might say, "Yes, I'm ready to go and have got the money available," and you say, "That's great, we'd like to use that and work with you." Then you go away for a week to sort out all the things out for the project, and you go back to the investor, and they say, "Well you went away, so we invested somewhere else." That happens quite frequently.

If somebody is ready to go and to invest, you need to understand what their drivers are and quite frequently it's wanting to get that money invested. They're only getting 1% per annum in the bank, and if it's still sitting there and another week goes by, they might get frustrated and want to look at alternatives. Regardless of what due diligence they've done, people do make rash decisions; they've overcome their fear of actually investing the money, and they see opportunities and sometimes take whichever one comes along. In that case, when you've got an investor potentially there, you've really got to look at whether you put the money into an Escrow account or some sort of separated account so that the money is physically there for you and can't be touched by the investor and be used for something else. Yes, that may mean you have another week or two or month of paying that investor interest, but at least you have the security of actually having that money there, available to use.

Making deals stick ...

Frequently, without any apparent reason either, and if you ask them they almost can't explain it, private investors just change their minds. You, therefore, have to look at ways of making sales stick.

This might take the form of engagement, asking questions, involving them in the process. Investors come in all shapes and sizes – sometimes they'll want to have an active interest in what you're doing, others are happy to give you the money and just get on with it. It depends on what type of investor you're working with to decide if one option is better than the other. Keeping them engaged and giving them a timeframe that you're working to; just saying, "I'll need the money soon," gives them no point of reference. "Soon," for you might be a month or two; "soon," for them might be tomorrow. This is why getting clarity is important such as, "What actions can we take?" or "Shall we get the paperwork sorted out so we're ready to transfer and go when we need to?" It's about engagement; it's about involvement; it's about talking people through the process so that they understand what's going on. Coming back to the word "transparency" again, we're sharing what we're doing and how we're doing it. Not maybe in huge detail, just relevant and appropriate for the private investors that you're working with.

Tell them: "In an ideal world, this is the date we'd like it to happen. What is preventing us from doing that? These are the steps we need to take to get us from where we are now to where we need to get. We need to get paperwork sorted, check for money laundering, and we need to go through the legal process. Do you have concerns or questions?" Just engage them in the process.

Railroading and how to avoid it

Occasionally, you'll find that people try to railroad you into doing something, and you're torn between feeling 'I need the money for this project' and knowing that someone is trying to railroad you into something you don't necessarily feel comfortable with. In this situation, you may need to decide whether it is better to walk away or to try and carry on negotiating.

You've got to marry this with your own values and what you feel comfortable with and go with your gut instinct. I don't think there's a right or wrong. But if you're being put under pressure by somebody to do something, you should assess whether you're comfortable with that and what your future relationship might be like. I've certainly been in situations in the past where I felt forced into doing something and got into a number of situations where because option A had happened, I didn't have any other alternative. So, I put myself in an ever-decreasing spiral. That's a scary place to be; when you've committed to doing something, and it then starts backfiring, and to reverse out of it is not necessarily easy. This is why I decided to start mentoring other property experts; to save them the pitfalls that I fell into.

It's at those times that you certainly need support and help. But the key thing is not to expose yourself to those types of situations in the first instance, and by doing everything properly, there's no reason why you should. I don't want to scare people off here. If you're doing things properly, and you're doing things in a structured way, there's no reason why you should expose yourself to unnecessary risk. That's one of the lessons that I've learned is that you need to understand where the control is and be comfortable with that.

Why it is worth the time and effort to get it right

Learning how to raise private finance is daunting, initially; in much the same way that learning to drive a car or learning to ski is going to feel scary if you've never done it before. However, the benefits of learning how to do this are massive.

The benefits of being able to work with other people's money are huge because it takes away the barriers of growing a portfolio if you do it correctly. If you've got to wait for your own earnings maybe to reach such a level that you can afford to do your next project, how long might it take you to grow a portfolio for the size of projects you can tackle? It might take you ten years. If you're working with investor finance, it's possible to massively, massively accelerate that process, and there's no reason why you shouldn't condense a ten-year plan into a two-year plan. So, what would that mean to you if you were able to do that? Everybody is going to be different with what their goals are, and it comes back to what your goals are. Effectively, you'll have an unlimited supply of finance available that will allow you to achieve pretty much whatever you want. So make your goals big!

Essentially, you will have an unlimited pot of money once you've learned the skills. Do we need an infinite amount of finance? Most people's goals and aspirations can be met with a relatively small amount of money. You don't need to be working with 50 different investors. If you've understood what you need in order to achieve the goals you need to achieve, you may find the actual amount of money you need in order to achieve that is relatively small. It may be that a couple of hundred thousand pounds would be more than adequate to achieve your goals. I think the perception is that you'll need so much money that that in itself is daunting because it seems such a big target. But actually when I'm working with clients and I look at, "How much do you need for your first project?" Frequently it's less than £50,000, so it's not an insurmountable amount of money. Yes, it can seem daunting the first time, but it's not so much money as to be out of the realm of possibility.

Recycling and reinvesting money – an exciting opportunity

Sometimes, investors will recycle – not necessarily all – some of the money out of a project. If the investor's got £50,000 in a project over 12 months and it goes well, and they get their money back after the 12 months, they might then be inclined to reinvest. They might also be inclined to tell their friends that they've had a positive experience and perhaps they'd like a slice of the action as well. I've had investors who have said, "Well I've got £100,000" – and if you look after them, now they haven't just got £100,000, maybe they have £200,000 or £300,000 available. They're testing the water a little bit with you in the first instance to see if they can work with you. So don't pre-judge anybody in terms of what they've got available. Don't overestimate how much you actually need to make progress, but you do need to be clear of the whole process and how you're going to exit from a loan and that particular deal; how is the investor going to get their funds back – and you need to be absolutely crystal clear right from the start.

"Regard your failures as learning experiences and research. Reflect on their benefit they will have shaped who you are today. Use this experience wisely, take responsibility for your actions."

164

It depends on the circumstances of the investor, but it's not uncommon for people to extend beyond the original agreement that might have been reached for a particular loan. Again, this is where the PR aspect of private finance comes in as you need to keep in touch with your investors and make sure that they're kept up to speed with where a particular project is. This also gives you an opportunity to see what the current thinking is of the investors as well, and what their appetite is for extending or coming into new deals. Just keep them informed of what you're doing. If you've got a stream of new deals coming through, and you've kept your investor happy, A: might they reinvest and B: might they tell their friends that they're getting a great deal, and they might be encouraged to also come and work with you. The PR aspect of it is really important to just keep people posted on what you're doing. Problems usually arise when you don't communicate well with your investors, so it's well worth keeping on top of. Once you've secured an investment, there's no reason why you shouldn't be able to reuse it multiple times.

Get Crystal Clear:

- Don't pre-judge anybody in terms of what they've got available.

- Don't overestimate how much you need to make progress,

- Be clear about the whole process

- Be clear how you're going to exit from a loan deal

- How is the investor going to get their funds back?

Anything is possible now …

So now you've read the book, you should have a very clear understanding of the importance of working with people, of understanding why people are important, why your own skills and your own uniqueness is a critical aspect of the journey that you're on now. You'll also understand the value of setting very specific goals that are achievable and how you can work on a step-by-step basis to achieve those goals. You'll understand just exactly what kind of projects are going to work for you to help you achieve those goals and whether they're one-year goals, five-year goals, 10-year goals; you'll understand that having set those goals and having a process that will help you achieve them, that now anything is possible.

You'll understand that it's vital to have proper professional guidance for certain aspects of the whole property investing journey, and that by getting proper professional help you'll actually save yourself both time and money and the embarrassment of not doing things right. You'll also understand the importance of taking care of your investors and the people who have a vested interest in the work that you're doing.

Hopefully, that will motivate you to continue taking action and to putting the skills that you've learnt in the book into action and actually going out there and working with investors and helping them to reach their goals.

Shelf Help

I think it's important when you read books like this that you don't just shove it on the bookshelf and forget about it. I have a great mantra in life if you're going to commit to doing something, "What's wrong with now?" You know, now is the best time to start making those changes and to start implementing what you've learnt. If you leave it, it gets diluted, and some other kind of priority fills the gap, and nature's really good at filling voids with other stuff. So make sure it's the right stuff.

You've learnt in this book what action to take: it's simple, it's systematic, and it's straightforward. Start taking action now. If it would help you to make contact with me to get motivation and accountability, I'm happy to look at that. It's important really that you drive this forward, that you take action, that you take responsibility for the rest of your life, and what better time to start than right now?

The power of action ...

When I'm coaching or mentoring clients, it's very much about them taking the action. I'm a keen sailor, and a sailing boat won't go anywhere without power of the wind. Given wind, you sail a sailing boat pretty much anywhere that you want to go, but without wind it will go absolutely nowhere. The story that I give to my clients is that if they provide that wind energy, I can help steer that boat for them to wherever they want to go. They are the ones providing the energy and the drive to achieve their goals; I'm simply guiding them and steering them to where they want to go to achieve their goals, so once we know where the goal is, and have the wind power to fill the sails, we can trim the sails then to achieve our destination.

Steps you can take in the next 10 minutes

Firstly, identify and articulate your reason why in very clear terms. The stronger and bigger WHY will help you better overcome adversity and challenges that you will encounter on your journey. Write it down, don't just think it. You may then go back and revisit it to add extra strength and depth as your passion for achieving it grows.

The next thing you need to do if you haven't done it already is to write a list of 30 things that make you unique and to understand that is something to be celebrated. I always challenge people if they say, "Oh, 30 things is a lot." Okay, so do 40. Don't stop at 30, keep going until you've got 40. Often, the last things that we think of are actually the most valuable, the most poignant. If you do struggle, ask friends, family, and people around you why they think people would come to you. What makes you unique? What makes you special? It will be different from absolutely everybody else, and it's really important to get that.

The next step that you can take is to identify what your goal is. Be really clear about what your goal is, whether that's a 12-month goal, or a five-year goal, whatever goal it is, to be really, really specific. Write down what that goal is and be very specific, very clear about what you're looking to achieve, and break it down into step-by-step elements that are actionable.

The next step that you can take is to work out what projects will help you, in an ideal world, achieve the goals that you've set out. So if the target is to achieve a passive income of £5,000 per calendar month, what does this look like in terms of the number of properties that you need to acquire in order to achieve that?

For example, take a situation where you've got perhaps an HMO that generates £1,000 cash flow per month. You would need five of those in order to get to the £5000 target; so how much money would be required for each of those five properties? Just break it down step by step, so that you understand exactly what you need to do to achieve your goals.

Then, identify the kind of investors that you would need to be working with to acquire the money, or to attract the money for those projects so that you can achieve those goals. If you start taking that action now, what's holding you back? You should be able to then take this and move forward very quickly because you're starting to create the butterfly garden that will attract the right people in to help you achieve your goals – because you've been very specific and very clear about what you want to attract into your life.

"We overestimate how much we can achieve in a day but underestimate what we can achieve in ten years. Keep taking the next step in the right direction. You will achieve amazing results."

Your brain will help you to achieve this, so you need to reflect on this regularly. If you've written it down, and you've got the opportunity to keep going back to it, you've got a framework to work to and to start taking action.

Often, it's great to have an accountability partner, somebody who will hold you accountable for achieving the goals and the milestones that you've set out.

Your complimentary free session

I am offering a first complimentary, free session for my readers to help give you an understanding of where you are now. This is because part of moving forward is understanding where you are at the moment. So we start to look at that and start to assess what you need to do in order to achieve your goals.

I'm looking to work with people who are prepared to put in the effort and the energy necessary to achieve these goals. I'm not really interested in working with people who need pushing too hard. I understand that you do need help and support because there are different levels of that, and it's important to understand that I can help the people most who put the most effort and energy into achieving those goals. This is not just another course. This is about taking massive steps towards achieving your goals and your desired outcomes.

FINANCIAL HEALTH CHECK
Where Are You Now?

To ensure you get the maximum benefit from this book, I recommend you make an assessment of where you are right now on your property journey. This will help you to focus on the really important things to help move you forward.

- **What are you currently doing in your life?**

- **What are you currently doing in your career or business?**

- **What have been your biggest successes in your life to date?**

- **What have been your biggest challenges in your life to date?**

- **What does success mean to you?**

- **What would you do with your time if you didn't have to work?**

- **How much passive income would you need to cover your living expenses?**

- **How much passive income would you need to be completely financially free?**

- **How much passive income would you need to be completely abundant?**

Financial Profile / Property Investment Goals

Where are you on your journey now?

Why have you chosen to invest in property?

Describe your existing property investment experience

- Current properties owned

  o Private Residential

  o Rented

  o Developments

  o Other

- Current values of the above properties

- Equity held in each property

- Mortgage details for the above properties

- Approx. Gross and Nett cash flow being achieved

- How could you increase the rental income from your existing portfolio?

- What have you done to achieve this?

- How much would you like to increase your income by?

Property Investing experience to date

- What experience do you have?

- Attitude to risk?

Where do you want to get to?

- What goals do you have currently?

- What do you think the biggest challenge is that you are facing right now?

- What are your priorities and challenges for the next 12 months?

- How many properties?

  - What type?

  - Monthly cash flow?

  - Level of equity / leverage?

  - What area?

  - What strategy is your main preferred strategy?

  - Second strategy?

  - Third strategy?

  - Why do you want this?

  - What will it give you?

  - What is preventing you?

What assets do you have available?

- How much capital do you have?
    - Savings
    - Pension
    - Equity in property
    - Investments
    - Other
    - What funds could you access over the next 90 days to invest?
- What age are you?
    - When do you want to achieve your goal by?
    - Why?
    - What will this give you?
- How much time do you have available to do property?
    - Per day
    - Per week
    - Per month
- What skills do you possess that will help with your property journey?
    - Skills I possess
    - Skills in my immediate power team
- What would one wish be for your property investment journey for the next 90 days?

DEFINE YOUR IDEAL INVESTOR

Being able to define your ideal investor will help you focus on that avatar and zone in to what makes them tick. Understanding this will enable you to better target your proposals and ensure you are dealing with people that you will enjoy working with. The late Terry Wogan was a master at understanding who his listener was, and he directed his whole show at that listener. It was very personal, and that is what made him so popular.

Remember you are not BEGGING for money, and you don't want to come across as NEEDY – this is presented as an OPPORTUNITY, which may or may not be appropriate for them at this given time.

Some of the criteria you may want to consider for this are:-

• How much experience do they have?

• *Have they invested with anyone before? Do they have any preconceptions? This may affect how they behave with you. What level of experience is ideal for you?*

• Are they familiar with property as a possible investment?

• *People who have invested in property and are familiar with what is possible may be looking for higher returns than people who are less familiar. This is a double edged sword. The more experience they have, the easier it will be to get them to invest; the payoff is they will expect a higher rate of interest. Non property people will be harder to win over but will not have such high expectations of how much interest they require. Indeed, if you go too high with the interest rate, this may actually put them off as it will be seen as being "too good to be true". How can you define this?*

- Do they invest in property already?

- *If not, you may have to educate them as you go; this can be a good thing but will take time. How could you turn this to your advantage?*

- Do they invest in other things, stock market, Forex, wine, etc.?

- *This will be an indicator as to their openness to explore different options. How can you use this to your advantage?*

- Are they hands-off investors?

- *What is the benefit to you if they are hands off? How would it affect your offer if they wanted guidance and a more hands on approach?*

- Do they want to get involved?

- *What could you offer them as an incentive to get involved?*

- How much available cash do they have?

- *Do you want someone who is giving up their life savings to your care? Do they have pension funds available? Are they aware of what they can do with pension funds? Who can you get to help you if they are interested in using pension funds?*

- What is their pain point?

- *Put yourself in their shoes? Is it low interest rates? Level of security? How can you use this?*

- How are you addressing this pain?

- *What are you doing that addresses their pain? How can you establish what their pain points are?*

- What is their attitude to risk?

- *How will this affect how you present the opportunity? Will you present differently to different risk profiles? How will you establish their attitude to risk?*

- What is their Talent Dynamics or Wealth Dynamics Profile?

- *Why are these very powerful tools? What will they tell you?*

- Are they detail oriented or big picture?

- *Why is this important? How will it affect your approach?*

- How long are they prepared to invest for?

- *What impact will this have on your strategy? How will you determine what works for the investor?*

- What interest rate will they be happy with?

- *Although you won't share this at first, why is it important to know what limits you are OK to work within?*

- What level of security will they look for?

- *What levels of security are you able to offer? If you are working with banks and other lenders, what are they happy with? They will want first charge, and many don't like you offering a second charge. How will you overcome this? What options do you have available?*

Add your own criteria that help give you greater clarity, such as location, age, gender, etc.

The clearer you can be, the easier it will be to focus in on the people you want to work with.

Remember you are not BEGGING for money, and you don't want to come across as NEEDY – this is presented as an OPPORTUNITY, which may or may not be appropriate for them at this given time.

DEFINE YOUR IDEAL PROJECT

Being able to define your ideal Project will help you focus on that avatar and zone in to attracting more of these types of deals. Understanding this will enable you to better target your proposals and ensure you are dealing with projects that meet your specific goals. The better you can get at understanding what makes your ideal project work, the easier you will find it to communicate that to your Ideal Investor.

Some of the criteria you may want to consider for this are:-

What is the ideal location?

- *Where will your project be?*

- *How is this influenced by your own location?*

- *What considerations will you make when choosing the location?*

Why is this location right?

- *What makes this the right location?*

- *What is the demand for rooms?*

- *What is the demand for sales?*

- *How strong is the local economy?*

- *What companies operate in this area?*

- *What is the employment situation?*

- *How much investment in the local economy?*

- *Who are your tenants going to be?*
- *How much will they pay?*
- *How good are transport links?*

What type of project is right for you?

- *BTL*
- *HMO*
- *Refurb/flip*
- *Flats*
- *Commercial to Residential*
- *Serviced Accommodation*
- *Rent 2 Rent*
- *Development*
- *Planning Gain*
- *Title Splitting*
- *Holiday lets*
- *Other?*

What value range fits your strategy?

- *Low end?*
- *Mid range?*
- *High end?*

What are the Risks of your particular strategy?

- Valuations
- Length of conversion
- Complexity
- Finance
- Planning
- Power team

What are your Numbers?

- What do your numbers need to look like so that the deal stacks?
- How quickly can you do the work?
- What is the impact of a delay?
- How quickly can you release finance?
- What are your exits?
- What are the risks attached to each exit?

Who is on your Power Team?

- Legal – conveyancing
- Legal – contracts
- Property Tax Accountant
- Mortgage and bridging finance broker
- Surveyor

- Architect / architectural technician

- Planning specialist

- Surveyor

- Project manager

- Letting agent

- Estate agent

- Builder

- Marketing

- Interior designer

- Coach / mentor

DISCLAIMER

The content, projections, figures and indications contained here in this book are based on opinion and cannot be relied upon when making investment decisions. As with any investment, property value can fall as well as rise.

The author offers this information as a guide only, and it cannot be considered as financial advice in any way. Please refer to your independent financial advisor who is qualified to give you complete advice based on your circumstances.

The author Tim Matcham is not qualified to give mortgage, legal, or financial advice. Please seek legal and financial advice from a qualified advisor before making commitments. Neither the author nor publisher accepts liability for decisions made based on the contents of this book.

This book is a guide only.

WORKING WITH ME

Like most things that require mastery, you can either do it all by yourself, or you can learn from other people that have already achieved the results you require. Modelling other successful people is one of the basic characteristics of effective business people.

Let's be quite clear here, as we're talking about dealing with other people's money, and you only get one chance to make an impression on someone, it would make a lot of sense to avoid as many mistakes as possible and spend your time, sweat, and resources working in the right direction.

For this reason, I provide select clients the opportunity to be mentored in order to maximise their chances of success, while minimising problems and costs incurred and shorten the overall length of time taken to achieve great results.

However, please understand that there is naturally only a finite amount of time available as I juggle other clients, projects, and my leisure activities. For this reason, there is currently a moderate waiting list for my services. <u>Check out my credentials, and you'll see why</u>.

Having raised over £2 million in the last couple of years, I know how stressful it can be … and how to do it properly!

Additionally, I need to guard my reputation as a coach that delivers on his promise and given that achieving the desired outcome is not trivial (many people are unable or unwilling to do what is required to attain results), I have to be very careful whom I accept as a client in the first place. For this reason, not all potential clients are accepted, and my services are subject to acceptance after a short initial phone-consultancy to determine suitability; for the benefit of all parties concerned.

Assuming we've had a consultancy (and likely a follow-up consultancy as well), and everything is favourable, you'll be invited to have a financial action plan.

WORKING TO A PLAN IS CRUCIAL

It should come as no surprise that your chances of success go through the roof when you work to a well-thought out and executed action plan. I insist on mapping-out this process for all my new clients because it gives everyone involved in the project a clear, structured 'roadmap' to work towards.

The benefits of working to a plan are many and varied, and the main ones include:

- **Clarity** : A structured approach is significantly more likely to succeed than an 'ad-hoc' one.

- **Communication** : Management of expectations (of all parties) is greatly improved.

- **Correction** : Objectives and milestones can be recorded, evaluated, and 'course adjusted' as necessary.

The process for developing the plan involves a four step process:

Step 1 - Fact Finding

As would be expected, this stage requires spending time with you (and any business partners you may have) for a comprehensive fact-finding process. I'll meet with you (in person or via webinar) for a couple of hours and go through a comprehensive set of questions which are specifically designed to elicit the information I need so that I can get right to the heart of the matter. (I'll need to know a lot of information about you and so if a non-disclosure agreement is required, this won't be an issue). This step underpins everything else and so can't be rushed. We'll look at the four key areas of Raising Private Finance. You will also have the opportunity of doing the Talent Dynamics Profile test and debrief.

Step 2 – Homework & Checklists

This is designed to get you thinking and sharing with me exactly what your reason why is, what makes you unique, your ideal deal and ideal investor. The checklists will guide you through, ensuring you provide me with the right information to help you progress, and of course what your goals and aspirations are.

Step 3 – Creating the Action Plan

This process will take me several hours and so I typically need between seven to ten working days in order to produce the document and fit it in my schedule. The plan is obviously bespoke and will take into account such considerations as were addressed in the previous two stages.

Step 4 - Delivering the Action Plan meeting

This is the moment of truth! We'll typically need a couple of hours together or via webinar where we'll go through every step of the action plan in detail. You'll have the opportunity to ask questions, challenge assumptions and/or suggestions plus ensure that the plan will meet your timescales, abilities and expectations.

Typically, I'll need to 'tweak' the action plan to accommodate any changes to the goals, budgets, timescales and activities that we agree to be appropriate after we've gone through it together. In this case, we'll organise another webinar to review the revised version together.

You will now be in possession of an action plan tailored for you which is a viable, workable document and <u>consequently very valuable to you</u>. It represents potentially hundreds of thousands of pounds (millions?) of future investment capital, when you implement it. Further to this, I can help offer ongoing training, coaching and guidance (if you require) in order to ensure that you remain on the path to success without wavering or getting lost. (i.e. you'll remain on the 'Blue Line' to success!)

Will IT Work?

Naturally, only you will know how much time and effort you're prepared to put into achieving your goals. All I can say is that without a doubt, the odds of achieving your goals and obtaining significant private finance are hugely increased by virtue of defining what the goals are in the first place (many people don't even get that far) and then working relentlessly towards a viable plan to achieve those goals and adjusting to feedback along the way.

In short, you're significantly more likely to succeed, but the results are ultimately down to your efforts – naturally.

Is There Any After-Care?

Yes! As part of the service, we'll have a follow-up session (again via webinar or in person) 30, 60, or 90 days after you've signed off the plan, depending on your circumstances, plus I'll be on hand to offer help according to the results you'll have achieved to that point. Furthermore, I also offer a monthly mentoring package where we can review your progress much more regularly (weekly, fortnightly, monthly, etc.), and this is a service that's only available to people that have undertaken the action plan for the reasons described at the outset.

How Long Are The Action Plans?

We (typically) work on an 180 or 365-day action-plan, depending on how quickly you wish to proceed, resources available to you, and your appetite for implementation!

What Other People Have Said

"Tim was very helpful on transition of our business when we were in overwhelm . He helped us prioritise, focus and communicate better, and seemed to have an army of helpful tools and techniques at his finger tips. A lovely calm and measured approach helped clarify issues and move us forwards."

John & Bronwen Vearncombe

"Tim's coaching is truly excellent, he has really helped me focus on what's important in my business. I'd say he's probably saved me 8 months worth of misdirected effort. His calm and considered style of coaching, coupled with his extensive knowledge and experience, is perfect for teasing the correct and most appropriate course of action out of you. He has certainly guided me away from the mass of detail and refocused my attention towards the end state. Even after a few sessions I have regained my focus and have a sound plan of action to achieve my goals. Highly recommended."

Grantley Clapham

(Full and original testimonials available upon request)

Yes, I'm Interested! What Do I Do Now?

Splendid! Simply contact me, and we can get things started.

Thank You!

Tim Matcham

Blue Line Coaching

tim@propertyfinance.coach

07792 707334

Made in the USA
Columbia, SC
14 October 2017